The implications for social security of structural adjustment policies

The implications for social security of structural adjustment policies

Studies and Research No. 34

International Social Security Association – Geneva

ISBN 92-843-1067-9

First published 1993

Also available in French and Spanish.

HD
7090
I 56
1993

Printed in Switzerland

Contents

Preface   *vii*

1   *The implications for social security of structural adjustment policies: An overview*   **1**

2   *Economic support in old age: The role of social insurance in developing countries*
James H. Schulz   **15**

3   *Structural adjustment and social security: The interaction*
Colin Gillion   **83**

4   *Toward a cost-effective social security system*
George Kopits   **103**

5   *Swiss Chilanpore: The way forward for pension reform?*
Dimitri Vittas   **113**

6   *Structural adjustment policies and their implications for social security in Latin America*
Rodolfo Saldain   **137**

7   *Implications for social security of structural adjustment policies: The point of view in French-speaking Africa*
Pierre Désiré Engo   **171**

8 **Implications for social security of structural adjustment policies in English-speaking Africa**
   Henry G. Dei   **177**

9 **A perspective from Central and Eastern Europe**
   Inara Bite   **183**

10 **The need for institutional reform**
    Stanford G. Ross   **187**

11 **Concluding comments**
    James H. Schulz   **193**

Preface

The implications for social security of structural adjustment policies were the focus of a Symposium organized on the occasion of the XXIVth General Assembly of the International Social Security Association in Acapulco, Mexico. Held in memory of Leo Wildmann, who served as Secretary General of the ISSA from 1949 to 1974, the Symposium provided a forum for international organizations and social security policy makers and administrators to exchange views on the role that social security programmes can play in the process of economic and social development.

This publication brings together the detailed reports written by the four keynote speakers in preparation for the Symposium, as well as the commentaries prepared by the five members of the panel of experts. The introductory chapter provides an overview of the proceedings and briefly summarizes the presentations of the keynote speakers, the comments of the panel members and the open discussion from the floor. The final chapter presents the concluding remarks made by Professor James H. Schulz in drawing the Symposium to a close.

1

The implications for social security of structural adjustment policies: An overview of the Symposium

On the occasion of its XXIVth General Assembly (22 November to 1 December 1992), the ISSA organized a Symposium in honour of the memory of Leo Wildmann, who served as Secretary General of the Association from 1949 to 1974. The aim of the Symposium was to provide a forum for the principal parties involved in social security and structural adjustment policies to present their views so that a better understanding could be reached of the role that social security can play in countries undergoing transformation of their economies and public finance policies.

The ISSA could see that there was an urgent need for an open and frank exchange on this issue. Such an exchange was all the more important since it concerned not only the majority of countries in Africa, Asia and Latin America, but also the emerging democracies in Central and Eastern Europe. In many of these countries, where significant structural reforms of their economies and public expenditures are taking place, social security programmes are often under threat. Social security officials in these countries see those responsible for formulating structural adjustment policies as being insensitive to the needs of the population, particularly in relation to minimum levels of income security and health protection. The proponents of structural adjustment policies counter such criticism with arguments about the level and distribution of benefits and the growing financial burden of benefits on state budgets. They suggest that greater emphasis on private sector approaches would increase programme equity and efficiency.

A number of critical issues are at the heart of this debate about the role of social security programmes in societies where significant transformation is occurring. It is widely recognized that social security can have important influences on the economy through, for example, sustaining consumer demand by replacing lost income during times of economic downturn, encouraging capital formation, and providing the basis for real economic growth by fostering a healthy and active working population. But, in view of the rapid economic changes that many countries are currently facing, it is time to re-examine how social security programmes can best contribute to the process of development. Which of the existing systems or what mix of different approaches is the most appropriate for countries facing rapid economic change? Under what circumstances are national social security systems more effective in promoting social equity than other approaches, including private initiatives?

Over the years, a variety of different approaches have evolved, depending on each country's priorities and different cultural and economic needs. The majority of countries have given prominence to different forms of statutory social protection, such as social insurance, complementary pension and health programmes, mutual benefits, provident funds and social assistance. Different countries, of course, have different mixes between public programmes and voluntary private schemes and different responsibilities between employers, workers and the state for financing the various forms of social protection. Furthermore, there is evidence that different countries attach quite different priorities to protection for different types of contingencies, such as income security in old age, health care, loss of employment and care of children.

The different approaches have been designed to meet the specific needs of different countries. But will they be able to adequately cope with the extent of change currently taking place? Will they need to be modified and reformed to meet newly emerging needs and social problems? And are cash benefits the most efficient mechanism for meeting these new priorities, or will assistance with housing, food and other basic needs also be required?

Inextricably linked to these economic and social issues is the broader debate about the responsibility of the modern state to prevent and alleviate poverty among its citizens. It is obvious that the market mechanism cannot meet the needs of every individual, but opinions vary as to the extent of the state's reponsibility to counteract the workings of the market place through, for example, the provision of basic health care, protection of the family and the promotion of individual human dignity.

The Leo Wildmann Symposium on the implications for social security of structural adjustment policies was organized to provide a forum for discussion of these issues which are of significance for national and international organizations involved in economic and social development throughout the world. It brought together social security programme administrators and experts from key international organizations to focus on the fundamental issues facing countries in economic and social transition. It was recognized, however, that the Symposium would represent only the beginning of a continuing dialogue which would be necessary to find answers to the questions which are not only of major importance to social security itself, but also for the successful implementation of economic adjustment policies in the various countries throughout the world.

The following represents a brief overview of the proceedings of the Symposium. It summarizes the addresses presented by the four keynote speakers from international organizations and the commentaries given by the five members of the panel of experts. It also provides a summary of the open discussion which took place following the formal presentations and presents a brief outline of the concluding remarks of Professor James H. Schulz.

Keynote speakers

The Symposium was opened by Mr Heribert Maier, Deputy Director General of the International Labour Office (ILO). He spoke about the valuable contribution which Leo Wildmann had made to the field of social security and particularly to the role of the ISSA during the post war period. He referred to a message from Mr Wildmann's daughters, thanking the ISSA Secretariat and Bureau for their innovative approach to honour the work of their late father. In introducing the keynote speakers and commentators, he mentioned that the ILO welcomed the changing attitudes of the International Monetary Fund (IMF) and the World Bank towards the integration of social protection into their economic development programmes.

The first speaker, Colin Gillion, Director of the Social Security Department of the ILO, examined the context in which structural adjustment programmes had developed. During the 1980s, many developing countries had faced a period of economic decline, brought about to some extent by external factors such as a deterioration in the terms of trade, high world interest rates and the consequences of monetary restraint in the industrialized countries. At the same time, however, the policies and structures of the developing countries were inappropriate to deal with these changed conditions. As a result, programmes of economic stabilization were introduced in an attempt to reduce, as quickly as possible, the large deficits and high rates of inflation. Other programmes were also introduced, with the long-term aim of changing the structure of these countries' economies to enable them to compete under market conditions. But these economic developments have had severe repercussions on social security and social protection programmes which have had to cope with increasing demands at a time when resources have diminished and urgent reform was already needed.

Mr Gillion therefore argued that social security programmes in developing countries should be restructured to respond to the social needs arising from the economic transition taking place. The immediate priority was to extend to the maximum degree possible the level of benefits and coverage of existing systems, but without endangering economic development. New and different programmes would be required to supplement traditional ones. They might take the form of basic income guarantees, with support from general revenue, as well as voluntary programmes with regulatory frameworks and close public supervision. Finally, many existing institutions would need to focus on administrative reform to ensure greater efficiency and effectiveness and provide greater transparency and accountability. In conclusion, Mr Gillion recognized that each country would have to meet its own needs and that there would be significant difficulties and constraints. But whatever the system implemented, it must deliver benefits effectively, efficiently and equitably.

The second speaker was George Kopits, Chief of the Fiscal Operations Division of the IMF, who spoke about the IMF's role in enhancing the cost-effectiveness of social insurance and social assistance schemes. He believed the social security crisis, while evident across a number of developing countries, was the most acute in the post-socialist economies of Central and Eastern Europe and the former Soviet republics, where ideological constraints were contributing significantly to the current problems.

In the second half of the 1980s, the IMF had changed its approach and began to address the social consequences of structural adjustment programmes, recognizing that without social and political acceptance, the viability of these programmes would be jeopardized. Initially, the IMF had focused on ways of strengthening the social safety net for adversely affected groups, but more recently, increasing attention was being placed on reforming permanent social security programmes. Since 1989, over 12 countries had received technical assistance in the design and administration of their schemes as well as assistance with temporary measures to alleviate poverty during the process of structural adjustment.

The viewpoint of the IMF was that social security systems should provide maximum protection with the minimum amount of resources and the least allocative distortions. There were therefore a number of considerations which should be taken into account in designing such a system. Mr Kopits listed these as being:

- the cultural and social characteristics, as well as the historical development of each country;

- the effects of the system on the allocation of resources and incentives to work and save;

- the level of economic development and labour market conditions;

- the need for clear institutional distinctions between social security schemes regarding function and purpose;

- the need for an equitable distribution of benefits and costs between present and future generations; and, finally,

- the speed with which reform can be implemented and the ability of the institutional framework to administer the scheme effectively.

The third speaker was Dimitri Vittas, Senior Financial Specialist from the World Bank. At the outset, he emphasized that there was no such thing as a World Bank view and that there could be no such thing as a perfect pension system. Even the best-designed system could not function without good government and good management and any system had to be flexible enough to cope with the uncertainties that the future might hold. Nevertheless, Mr Vittas put forward for consideration a blueprint for pension reform. His system, called "Swiss Chilanpore", was based on the best features of the pension systems in Switzerland, Chile and Singapore. He chose these countries because each of them had a compulsory, substantially funded system covering all workers and a successful economy with high levels of national and household saving.

The system proposed by Mr Vittas was a multi-pillar system, comprising two compulsory pillars and one or two voluntary ones. The government would have the responsibility to ensure that not only the compulsory pillars functioned properly, but also that the voluntary pillars were regulated and supervised fairly.

The first pillar would be based on the Swiss first pillar — a flat-rate, full-career minimum pension and a partial earnings-related pension. A social assistance scheme could provide benefits for those with insufficient means. The pension system would be financed on a pay-as-you-go basis with contributions of between 5 and 10 per cent. The second pillar, similar in structure to the Chilean system, would be a defined contribution plan with individual capitalization accounts, financed by contributions of between 10 and 15 per cent. However, to avoid the high level of operating costs that was an undesirable feature of the Chilean system, this pillar would be administered through a central agency. The investment of pension funds would be entrusted to authorized and well-regulated private companies.

Voluntary pension schemes could also be established either by employers or by individuals wanting higher replacement ratios than those provided under the compulsory pillars. These would also need to be regulated to protect the interests of consumers, so that there would be provisions for vesting and portability as well as guidelines for the investment of funds.

In conclusion, Mr Vittas stressed the importance of creating a system that was based on the principles of solidarity and redistribution, operating and investment efficiency and the accumulation of sufficient balances for the payment of adequate but affordable pensions. His proposed system envisaged a continuing but reduced role for public pensions and a much reduced role for company-based pension schemes.

The fourth speaker, James Schulz, Consultant to the ISSA and Professor of Economics at Brandeis University, focused on why social insurance had become the major form of social protection throughout a variety of different countries and why it was so important when more and more countries were moving towards market economies. He listed its strengths as:

- its ability to spread risks and provide for the social needs of different groups in the population;

- its guarantee of long-term programme viability and economic security of individuals regardless of their changing circumstances;

- its effectiveness in complementing family support without destroying family values and its avoidance of means-testing; and

- its avoidance of complex investment decision-making required by individual and group saving schemes.

Nevertheless, social insurance programmes had been the subject of growing criticism in developing countries because of limited coverage, administrative mismanagement, benefit inequities and resource deficiencies. But one should examine these problems in the context of other options available to policy makers, the main ones being the family, social assistance, employer-based schemes and savings schemes. Families and social assistance should remain an important part of social networks but they should not become the major focus for meeting the income security needs of the population. The limitations of family support were increasing as the traditional agricultural economy declined, while social assistance schemes were stigmatizing, politically vulnerable, costly to administer and discouraged labour force participation and individual saving. Employer-sponsored pensions had become subject to increased government regulation to protect workers, thereby increasing the administrative costs and the complexity of these schemes and decreasing the incentive for employers to extend coverage. With regard to personal savings, there was a fundamental problem that individuals would always undersave for their old age. The complexities of the financial market and the inability to obtain index-linked securities were further disadvantages.

Nevertheless, Professor Schulz emphasized that the provision of economic security through social insurance programmes relied on trust. Without trust, the viability of any programme would be seriously undermined, resulting in individuals and groups seeking special consideration and benefits at the expense of others. Hence, there was a need for an effective set of mechanisms for reviewing the general operations of each programme and assessing its financial integrity. In many developing countries, the financial conditions of the social insurance programmes had deteriorated to a point where they were no longer viable. Thus, interest in fundamental changes to the current systems was beginning to emerge. Professor Schulz, however, while appreciating the need for a multi-pillar approach, argued that social insurance, based on universalism, should continue to be the foundation for any system designed to meet the income security needs for old age.

Comments by panel of experts

The first commentary was presented by Rodolfo Saldain from Uruguay. While recognizing the necessity of structural adjustment policies for budgetary discipline, reducing inflation and opening up opportunities for foreign trade and investment, he believed that the IMF and the World Bank tended to argue for the imposition of certain set proposals without any consideration of individual countries' political and social situations.

Social security in Latin American countries had been characterized by severe budgetary imbalances, leading in some cases to financial crises. This was due to a certain extent to political inaction which had resulted in a significant decline in the real value of benefits. It was therefore obvious that social security programmes required financial and actuarial viability, but the question was who should lead the process of reform — social security managers or those implementing structural adjustment policies. If, however, it were the social security managers, they must abandon their "romantic" discourse and start discussing issues in financial and economic terms. At the same time it was most important that social security programmes retained their social objectives and did not become entirely based on economic premises. That institutional reform was required was not in contention, but this did not automatically mean that social security should become a capitalization scheme administered by private managers. What was needed was cooperation between the public and private sectors and discussions about the appropriate role for each of them. Social security should become depoliticized and not, as had happened in the past, be simply used to collect votes.

In conclusion, Mr Saldain stressed the need for social security reform to be oriented towards social protection, extending coverage as much as possible but avoiding any dysfunctionality. Because structural adjustment programmes were socially hazardous, social security would be called upon to play an even more important role than it had done previously.

Stanford Ross, a former Commissioner of the Social Security Administration in the United States, stressed the need to increase awareness of the limitations of social security. It was all too easy for governments to make too many promises that could not be met because of institutional constraints. In his view, incrementalism, rather than fundamental change, was the best approach to the reform or development of social security systems. There should be long-term strategic plans outlining goals for the future and the processes for implementation.

In this context, Mr Ross believed that the ISSA had a very important role to play in advising member organizations on management technology and informing them of the experiences of others. Good quality management was essential for the functioning of any social security programme. Mr Ross concluded his remarks by emphasizing that it was better to develop systems that were perhaps limited in scope but which could deliver what had been promised, not less. He also urged that a more balanced approach was needed, with governments, employers, institutions and individuals cooperating to achieve a better system of social protection for the population.

Pierre Désiré Engo from Cameroon focused on his country's experiences with the effects of structural adjustment programmes. Even though less than 20 per cent of the active population in Cameroon was covered by social security, these people were the first victims of the cutbacks in public expenditure that had been prescribed under the structural adjustment programme. An immediate consequence was the loss of 30,000 jobs. Salaries were also frozen, with the result that there was a loss in productivity and an increase in corruption and fraud. For those not in formal employment, there was a further increase in poverty. The reduction in social expenditure meant that children could no longer go to school, and access to health care and decent accommodation declined. It was quite apparent that economic measures had been confused with social measures and that there was a total lack of understanding by the IMF and the World Bank of the social consequences of their policies.

To give a specific example of the effects of structural adjustment, Mr Engo discussed the changes which had been introduced within the National Social Insurance Fund. Whereas previously the Fund had been able to build up reserves, it was now in deficit, despite the fact that its objectives had been completely re-oriented towards financial profitability. Other examples were cited — the eventual privatization of health and social services which would tend to exclude a large section of beneficiaries; the suggestion that family allowances should be deducted from employers' contributions, which was totally against the principle of independence between worker and employer in relation to benefits; the suspension of reimbursement of medical expenses during pregnancy, which was in conflict with the minimum standards of social security; and the suppression of the right to family allowances for children born outside a legal marriage which ignored the demographic realities within many African countries.

Mr Engo concluded his comments by indicating that he welcomed this opportunity for cooperation between the international agencies in their efforts to help developing countries, but at the same time urged that the countries themselves should have a right to be heard in the formulation of plans for reform.

The viewpoint of the former socialist economies was presented by Inare Bite from Latvia. She emphasized that the transition to a market economy placed a heavy burden on social security systems as unemployment increased, the real value of benefits fell and administrative difficulties arose because of the need to set up a safety net to assist the most vulnerable groups.

Ms Bite indicated that in most of the central and eastern European countries, social security systems were being transformed into statutory social insurance schemes, not simply to copy western practices, but because of a belief in the basic principles of social insurance, particularly the financing from contributions by employees and employers. All of these countries had had bitter experience with benefits being paid out of state budgets. Although they were endeavouring to follow the recommendations of the IMF and the World Bank, there were significant difficulties to be faced. The psychological effects of introducing flat-rate pensions, for example, meant that workers who had had expectations of earnings-related pensions were disillusioned, resulting in an increase in social tension within the community. Furthermore, the suggestion to increase pensionable ages must be seen in the context of relatively low average life expectancy (in Latvia, the average life expectancy for men is 62) and the increasing levels of unemployment, while the proposal to calculate pensions on the basis of wages during the entire working life could not be implemented before significant improvements were made to the administrative recording system. Ms Bite therefore warned that what might be the economically cheapest course might ultimately be of great social cost.

The final commentary was given by Henry Dei, from Ghana. He focused his comments on how structural adjustment programmes should be reformed to become sustainable in the long term. One of the major problems with such programmes was that they resulted in retrenchments, thereby immediately increasing the number of beneficiaries while reducing the number of contributors. In Ghana it had become apparent that structural adjustment programmes had not addressed a number of basic issues, such as the need to improve the agricultural yield by peasant farmers, the provision of basic, rather than expensive, high level training for the majority of the workforce, improvements in infrastucture and communications, the provision of functional housing and the extension of social security to rural areas.

Mr Dei stressed that, during the process of economic development, social security should become independent from state finances and operate on a self-sustaining basis. It should also, through the investment of funds, provide the basis for implementing long-term development plans in conjunction with the private sector.

Open discussion

In opening the discussion from the floor, the Secretary General of the ISSA, Dalmer Hoskins, drew attention to the evolution of social protection policies over the past century. There had been significant developments, from small-scale social assistance programmes and charity to assist the destitute to full-scale social insurance programmes covering all employees. The debate over structural adjustment policies had focused attention on what the appropriate foundation for social security should be in the future and what the appropriate mix should be between public and private responsibilities. It was most important that we should focus on how social security can facilitate, rather than hinder, economic development and how social protection can be attuned to the level of economic and social development of the country.

The contributions from the floor were quite diverse and included outright rejection of the IMF/World Bank structural adjustment programmes, a strong defence of social assistance policies, the continuing need for solidarity in the provision of social protection and discussion of the appropriate role for the ISSA. It was apparent, however, from all the contributions, that the delegates welcomed this opportunity for an exchange of ideas between the key players in such an important area.

The first speaker focused his remarks on the practical assistance which should be provided to countries in transition. France had already started assisting French-speaking African countries, but there was scope for expansion of the programme to other regions, with the ISSA taking on responsibility for its coordination. Another delegate from France indicated that there was a lack of international solidarity accompanying the implementation of structural adjustment programmes. These programmes, which essentially meant austerity for large categories of the population, were usually left to economic and financial experts, and consequently there was little focus on the social implications.

A delegate from a former socialist country emphasized that it was very difficult for outsiders to understand the problems faced by economies in transition. Hungary had had a well-developed social security system which enjoyed a great deal of popular support, but with the decline in living standards, the social tensions and the many changes that were occurring, the insured population were losing confidence in it. There was, moreover, concern that in the process of structural adjustment, the important principle of solidarity was being lost, and that social security was becoming a compulsory system along the lines of private enterprise.

Strong support for social assistance was expressed by a delegate from Australia. That country's system of social security, which was based on flat-rate, means-tested benefits, had existed for 90 years and was supported by all sectors of society, including employers and trade unions. Whereas social insurance was limited in terms of the contingencies it could effectively cover, social assistance could cover all types of risks, including unemployment and sole parenthood. The issue of adverse incentives often associated with means-testing was important in theory but there was little empirical evidence despite many years of academic research. Social assistance also provided governments with greater flexibility, in terms of both the vertical redistribution of income and administration. He therefore favoured an approach for developing countries whereby there would be social assistance to deal with unemployment and poverty, funded employer-sponsored schemes (which, in the longer-term, could become social insurance schemes) and a third tier comprising supplementary savings.

After six years of structural adjustment policies in Nigeria, the result had been high rates of inflation, devaluation of the currency and continuous reviews of salaries leading to strikes, riots and general disorder. This delegate saw structural adjustment as being synonymous with privatization, commercialization and withdrawal of government participation. If he were given responsibility for implementing a new social security system, he would adopt a social insurance scheme with indexed benefits and pay-as-you-go financing, thereby minimizing the worst effects of inflation. He would also advise against any structural adjustment programme.

A delegate from India sought clarification from the IMF of the phrase "structural adjustment", why it was thought that social security hindered economic growth and to what extent there should be government intervention. With the increase in unemployment associated with the withdrawal of the public sector and with no social protection, it would seem that there would be new social tensions and unrest, requiring more (unproductive) expenditures on law and order. Social security might be unproductive from a conservative viewpoint, but at least it acted as a "shock absorber", cushioning the adverse effects of market economies.

In response, Mr Kopits indicated that structural adjustment programmes were a necessary evil for those countries which had been operating with closed economies and structural rigidities. Nevertheless, neither the IMF nor the World Bank had any precise formula which they wished to impose on governments. They were aware that the most important aspects were a programme's sustainability and affordability, and this meant that programmes had to be adapted to take into account each country's cultural and social institutions. He also indicated that the IMF was learning from its experience, particularly in Ghana, and that a programme always had a greater chance of success if the initiatives came from the country itself and the administrators were involved in the design of the programme. Another interesting comment was that he felt that, in many cases, those in charge of the structural adjustment programme in each country - usually the Department of Finance or the Central Bank - were not in touch with the social security administrators. It was essential that internal dialogue be established and that a broad consensus be established between the government and the people.

Mr Kopits then made a few comments about retirement ages for pension eligibility. In his view, the retirement age should be flexible, but based on actuarially sound predictions. In some cases, early retirement might be justified, for example, in those occupations such as coal mining where life expectancy was lower than average. Any increase in the age of retirement should, of course, be phased in gradually. In conclusion, he emphasized that his argument was not that social security hindered economic growth, but that a cost-effective system was necessary for the achievement of sustained economic growth.

The discussion continued with the Secretary General of the European Institute of Social Security raising a point which he felt had tended to be overlooked so far — that social security was a human right guaranteed by international conventions and most national constitutions and that it therefore could not be easily disposed of. Another point raised by this delegate involved the fact that economists always looked at things from the viewpoint of the enterprise. In this case, social security was clearly a cost, but what was often forgotten was that, as with all other costs, it was also an income which added to the economy.

The final contribution from the floor gave an example of a positive outcome from the implementation of a structural adjustment programme. In the Dominican Republic, the social security system had contributed to over 50 per cent of the government deficit and should have been restructured 15 years earlier. Under guidance from the World Bank, certain changes had been introduced, including an increase in retirement age and modification of the pension formula. The speaker urged the panel to consider putting forward a recommendation that experts in social security should be involved in the drawing up of structural adjustment programmes.

Concluding remarks

Professor Schulz was then called upon to summarize the discussion and present concluding remarks. He focused on three basic issues — extending coverage, adequacy and equity, and implementation. The extension of coverage, he felt, had received the least attention during the Symposium and yet it was becoming more important than ever. Although this question had been looked at many times over the years, it was time for the ISSA to once again consider it in a very serious way. In discussing the issue of adequacy and equity, Professor Schulz drew attention to the two main approaches which were currently being suggested — increased targeting among government programmes and the establishment of a multi-pillar system. Despite the popular support enjoyed by the social assistance scheme in Australia, Professor Schulz believed that the expansion of the more typical social assistance programmes would involve serious incentive problems. With regard to the establishment of a multi-pillar approach, there were differences of opinion on where the emphasis should be in relation to the pillars, but a number of speakers had stressed the importance of good government for the successful operation of each of the pillars. Consequently, Professor Schulz's view was that the distinction between public and private tended to become somewhat blurred. There had also been two main approaches discussed during the Symposium in relation to implementation and the problems involved in making programmes more efficient and effective. One was privatization with government regulation; the other was to push for greater openness with regard to the operation of government-run programmes. It seemed that both of these approaches were appropriate and could be followed simultaneously with regard to the various pillars.

In conclusion, Professor Schulz stated that there was no global answer to the question that the Symposium had sought to address and that it was now time to move from the general to a more specific analysis of the issues. This was, of course, a major concern for the ISSA and he hoped that the Symposium represented only the beginning of the dialogue on this very important topic.

2

Economic support in old age: The role of social insurance in developing countries

James H. Schulz
Professor at Brandeis University (United States) and ISSA Consultant

Table of Contents

Economic security for the elderly — 18

The response of nations — 18

Time to assess and rethink approaches — 21

What role for social insurance? — 22

An overview — 24

Other mechanisms — 24

The family — 25

Key support from families — 26

Families remain important — 27

Changes in developing countries? — 27

The size problem — 29

Social assistance | 31
Employer-sponsored pensions | 35
Voluntary and compulsory savings plans | 41

The origins of social insurance | 47

Rising interest in pensions | 48
The rationale for collective action | 49
Security in large numbers | 51
Why compulsory pensions? | 52
How appropriate for developing countries? | 54
The "Welfare State" | 55
Does history repeat itself? | 58

Developing countries today: The reality and the challenge | 61

What benefits? For whom? | 62
The coverage problem | 64
Adequacy issues | 67
Equity | 68
Informed participation | 70
Implementation and administration | 70
Skill and training deficiencies | 71
High administrative costs | 72
Contribution avoidance | 72
Low returns on reserves | 72
Dishonesty | 73
Competition and privatization | 73
Economic issues | 76
Savings | 77
Labour supply disincentives | 78

Trust: The foundation of social insurance | 79

Acknowledgements | 82

Economic support in old age: The role of social insurance in developing countries

In recent years social insurance programmes in many developing countries have come under sharp attack. Major issues have been raised with regard to how these programmes are operating, especially with regard to problems of inadequate coverage, adequacy and equity, shortfalls in financing, and administrative mismanagement. In addition to discussing these problem areas, this chapter reviews the major social insurance options: the family, social assistance, employer-sponsored pensions, and savings plans encouraged or operated by governments.

At the heart of economic welfare for individuals around the world are matters of economic *growth*, conditions of *survival*, and the distribution of *risks*. All nations seek to promote and increase the welfare of their people through the expansion of food, housing, goods, and services (i.e., through economic growth). And, while many factors influence or determine the rate of growth, there is general recognition that human behaviour as it affects productivity and risk-taking is critical and, therefore, that appropriate incentives for work must be maintained. At the same time, there is recognition that the human condition is all too often one of immiserization and premature death, demanding interventions that may be antithetical to the economic growth objective.

Thus, over the years there has been a continuing debate over the extent to which individuals — confronted by a variety of economic opportunities, economic changes, and economic risks — should be responsible for their own welfare or should receive social protection from private or government collectivities. As observed by Theodore J. Lowi, "the welfare state is a recent effort to solve the ancient and perennial problem of how to save people from starvation without lowering their incentive to work."[1]

This debate continues in most countries today — over who should receive social protection, the extent of the protection, and how it should be provided. Work, because of the economic output it helps to produce and the claims on output it generates, plays a central role in the debate. On the one hand, it is a

---

1. Theodore J. Lowi. "Risks and Rights in the History of American Governments," *Daedalus*, vol. 119 (Fall 1990): pp. 17-40 (p. 25).

key factor for generating economic welfare for all; on the other hand, its cessation threatens the survival of particular individuals.

Economic security for the elderly

This paper focuses on the elderly, many of whom do not work. The problem of economic provision for people in their old age has confronted all societies throughout history. In the absence of special provisions for distributing the output of society, the economic security of people everywhere (including the elderly) is threatened when any of the following events occur:

- temporary interruption of working ability because of the unavailability of jobs (i.e., unemployment), short-term injury, and sickness;[2]

- longer disruptions in work capacity arising out of developmental disabilities, inadequately developed personal or vocational skills, obsolescence of on-the-job capacities, or age discrimination; and

- permanent interruption of the ability to work because of old age, permanent disability, or death.

While individuals of all ages are subject to these problems, the incidence of these occurrences *rises dramatically with age.*

Today, in addition, many nations find the problems enumerated above compounded by other factors: (a) Dramatically larger numbers of people are forced to retire (or are opting to retire) at much earlier ages, resulting in a growing segment of the population that spends much longer periods out of the labour force. (b) At the same time, there has been no significant decrease in the extremes in income and wealth inequality throughout the world that are a by-product of efforts to increase economic output — making retirement provision extremely difficult (if not impossible) for many low-income individuals. (c) Adding to the difficulties is the fact that traditional family support systems for the elderly have come under increasing stress as economic development proceeds.

The response of nations

In response to these old and new problems, nations have developed a rich array of cultural traditions, interpersonal mechanisms, and collective pro-

---

2.   A special problem confronting younger women is the temporary disruption of work patterns as a result of childbirth.

grammes. To provide an overview of historical developments, we group the variety of collective mechanisms into nine general categories:[3]

- *Social assistance*: Cash benefits are provided by religious orders, charities, and/or governments to individuals who can demonstrate that they meet specified eligibility criteria associated with defined categories of need. "Means tests" are typically applied to their income and/or assets as one condition of eligibility.

- *Mutual benefit societies*: Occupational or industrial groupings of members are organized under principles of solidarity among members to provide mutual aid in times of need. Benefits are provided through contributions paid by members with decisions made by the members collectively. Current mutual benefit societies often operate under the supervision or regulation of government ministries or regulatory agencies. Around the world today, there are large numbers of mutual benefit societies, insurance companies operating on mutual benefit principles, and a growing number of agricultural mutual benefit organizations.

- *Social services*: All nations provide various types of in-kind or non-cash benefits. Common examples are medical care, homemaker, handyman, and home-meal services; adult day-care centers; coping advice, information, and referral services; and special transportation. In some countries these benefits are provided only on a means- or income-tested basis, and in others there are user-fees.

- *Employer liability programmes*: Employers are often *required by law* to provide designated benefits to their employees and/or dependents either directly or under an approved insurance policy. The most common of these programmes throughout the world today are employer work injury insurance programmes.

- *Occupational and industrial pension programmes*: Retirement, survivor, and disability payments, either periodic or lump-sum, are paid out by employers or unions who take principal responsibility for administering special pension plans. Payments are conditional on a specified employment record and a variety of other factors (such as age or occupational disability). These

---

3. For greater detail on the options see, for example, John Dixon. *Social Security Traditions and Their Global Applications* (Canberra: International Fellowship for Social and Economic Development, 1986) or Ehtisham Ahmad. "Social Safety Nets," in Vito Tanzi, ed. *Fiscal Policies in Economies in Transition* (Washington, DC: International Monetary Fund, 1992), pp. 312-329.

benefits are usually encouraged by governments through special tax incentives and, in a few countries, have been mandated.

- *Savings incentive programmes*: These programmes seek to *encourage* individuals to save for their future economic security. Governments sometimes provide tax subsidies on monies invested in "retirement accounts," and employees sometimes match contributions in company-sponsored programmes. Usually these accumulations cannot be withdrawn without substantial penalties until a specified age. Typically, the resulting savings accumulation can be either withdrawn in a lump sum and/or used to purchase an annuity to meet continuing needs in old age.

- *Compulsory savings programmes*: Government administered programmes, called provident funds, are common in South-east Asia and Africa. Employers (and often workers) are required to make regular payments into a publicly administered or supervised fund. These payments are credited to a separate account maintained for each employee. While the money is being held in these accounts, interest or dividends arising from investment of the principal are credited. The accumulated sum is payable in a lump sum in accordance with specified payout criteria — most commonly at old age but sometimes to purchase housing, to meet the costs of serious illness, or a variety of special needs (such as a marriage dowry).

  In Chile and Mexico, and under consideration in other Latin American countries, are national compulsory savings programs for various workers that are administered in large part by non-government organizations. In Chile, covered workers select a private investment company from a list of government-approved organizations. Using the principal and investment return accumulated in individuals' accounts, these companies provide workers with old age, disability, and survivors' benefits. The government closely supervises all aspects of the process and provides certain guarantees to participating individuals regarding minimum benefits.

- *Social allowances or universal (demogrant) programmes*: Periodic benefits are provided to all elderly residents or citizens without respect to income, employment, or other means.

- *Social insurance*: National pension programmes have been legislated and are administered by (or are under the supervision of) the government — providing periodic cash payments for unemployment, old age, death, survivor's needs, disability, sickness or maternity, work injury, and/or the birth of a child.

Time to assess and rethink approaches

The experience of the past, emerging trends, and fears about the future have combined to generate a clear need for nations around the world to reassess their approaches to income maintenance in old age:

- In industrialized countries, the steady ageing of populations and the unusual circumstances created by the retirement of the "baby boom" populations during the early part of the 21st century have combined to raise new questions and concerns about financing "the welfare state."[4]

- While demographic ageing, until recently, was viewed as a phenomenon primarily affecting industrialized countries, it has become clear that this is too simplistic a view. "Aging is now a global problem, affecting developing countries as well."[5] Projections indicate that many developing countries are ageing more rapidly than was the case for the currently industrialized world and that the numbers of older people in these countries who will need economic support will, in absolute numbers, be much larger (at a time when pressures on families are increasing). As the United Nations points out, the central policy implication of the changing situation "is that developing regions of the world will have to plan for the increasingly rapid ageing of their populations."[6]

- The rapid economic growth of the immediate post-World War II period gave way to slower growth and periods of stagnation in the 1970s and 1980s. Oil price increases, recurrent inflation and recession, increasing deficits and growing debt burdens, high unemployment, growing "informalization" of labour forces, and stagnant (sometimes declining) real wages were among the many new economic developments in various countries throughout the world. The result was new strains on the financing of social programmes and growing fears about financing in the future. In many developing countries there has been a need to institute difficult programmes of economic stabilization and structural adjustment — often with the assistance of international

---

4. See, for example, Alan Pifer and Lydia Bronte, eds. *Our Aging Society: Paradox and Promise* (New York: W. W. Norton, 1986); Ben J. Wattenberg. *The Birth Dearth* (New York: Pharos Books, 1987); James H. Schulz, Allan Borowski, and William H. Crown. *Economics of Population Aging: The "Graying" of Australia, Japan, and the United States* (New York: Auburn House, 1991).

5. United Nations. *The World Ageing Situation 1991* (New York: United Nations Office at Vienna, Centre for Social Development and Humanitarian Affairs, 1991), p. 21.

6. Ibid.

agencies. Again, questions and fears have been raised about the future of existing social programmes, including programmes for the elderly.

• Even if there had been no major changes in population demography or the economic situation, there would still be rising concerns today about providing economic support to the elderly in developing countries. Unlike in the industrial countries, where government programmes supporting the elderly are viewed as a great social protection success story of the post-war period, there has been growing criticism and skepticism with regard to aged income maintenance programmes in developing countries.[7] Varying from country to country, there have been a variety of concerns — such as limited coverage, administrative mismanagement, benefit inequities, inflation devaluation, funding inadequacies, work and saving disincentives, and the possibility of fiscal drag on government budgets from mushrooming (sometimes overly liberal) programme expenditures.

What role for social insurance?

Of the nine categories listed above, social insurance is clearly the most important source of income for the elderly in almost all industrialized countries and is a growing source of income in many developing countries. While each country has a unique history with regard to the development of social insurance, a high degree of commonality has emerged over time among the programmes. Today, most social insurance programmes have:

• compulsory participation;

• benefits related to earnings levels and/or length of employment (sometimes complemented by a flat rate, more universal benefit);

• contributory taxes levied on both employers and workers, often supplemented by general revenues from government;

• benefits designed to meet "minimum income needs" during the retirement period;

---

7. See for example, C. Mesa-Lago, ed. *The Crisis of Social Security and Health Care: Latin American Experiences and Lessons* (Pittsburgh, PA: University of Pittsburgh Press, 1985); William McGreevey. *Social Security in Latin America — Issues and Options for the World Bank*, World Bank Discussion Papers, 110 (Washington, DC: the International Bank for Reconstruction and Development/World Bank, 1990); Kye Woo Lee. "Financing of Social Security: New Perspectives in Light of Current Economic Developments." Paper given at the ISSA Fifth American Regional Conference, Ottawa, 8-11 October, 1991.

- benefits that are an "earned right," to be received without a means test (usually, with some redistribution of income to groups among the elderly viewed as particularly needy); and

- benefits paid out regularly (e.g., monthly) till death, with the resultant financial obligations based on insurance principles that allow for the pooling and sharing of risk.

While the convergence among plans in various countries is impressive, one should not underestimate the variations that also exist. As Wilensky has observed, "we find momentous differences [among public pensions] in welfare effort, in program emphasis, in administrative style, and in the politics of welfare."[8]

With the growth of these social insurance programmes there has been increasing concern about how well they are performing and whether, given continuing problems and rising costs, there should be major cutbacks or perhaps elimination of certain programmes. It would be incorrect to characterize the recent criticisms of and debates about social insurance as primarily discussions of whether these programmes should be abolished and what to put in their place. The main debate in most countries has been about the importance of social insurance as an income maintenance mechanism in relation to the other options. That is, discussion has not focused on choosingthe "one best" mechanism to provide support to the elderly; rather, the focus has been on selecting an appropriate mix of different programmes or mechanisms and on the relative advantages of public and private approaches. In Western Europe this discussion has taken on a special dimension in recent years as the countries of the European Community (EC) seek to find ways to better coordinate their different social security programmes.[9] Given the numerous unresolved issues in many developing countries (where there has been less success in the past), the discussions about the future of social insurance are more complicated and the outcomes less certain. In fact, in Latin America and Eastern Europe, there have been some major changes.[10]

---

8. Harold L. Wilensky. Preface to the Japanese edition of *The Welfare State and Equality: Structural and Ideological Roots of Public Expenditures* (Tokyo: Bokuta Kusha, 1984), p. 3.

9. See, for example, Heinz-Dietrich Steinmeyer. "Harmonisierung des Arbeits- und Sozialrechts in der Europaischen Gemeinschaft: Eine Konsequenz aus der Schaffung eines einheitlichen Binnenmarktes?" *Zeitschrift fur auslandisches und internationales Arbeits- und Sozialrecht* Vol 3 (July-September 1989): pp. 208-228; Winfried Schmähl. *Harmonization of Pension Schemes in Europe? A Controversial Issue in Light of Economies*, Working Paper #7191 (Bremen, Germany: Zentrum für Sozialpolitik, Universität Bremen, 1991).

10. For example, the introduction of compulsory savings schemes in Chile and Mexico.

An overview

In the sections that follow, we argue that economic development is accompanied by new sources of economic insecurity that threaten the social welfare of individuals. The constant "economic revolution" generated by competition and markets promotes economic efficiency and growth but, at the same time, generates widespread social chaos. Too often policy advisers (especially economists) give great weight to the long-term gains of markets but little weight to the short-term misery created in the process. Politicians cannot long ignore these problems, however; social problems are the source of political instability (and, in the extreme, revolution).

The key question is *not* whether there should be a variety of social programmes instituted during the development process. Social programmes to moderate the worst results become a necessity, given the clearly limited ability of individuals and their families to fully cope with the problems created. The critical question that needs to be addressed is *what combination of programmes* should be started at various stages of the development process?

Historically, social insurance has played a major role, together with the family, in providing this vital social protection. The dominant role played by social insurance is no accident. Social insurance combines the techniques of actuarial risk-spreading and financing of private insurance with the social adequacy ("solidarity") and long-term security (viability) resulting from spreading eligibility across the population and creating meaningful guarantees backed by the government's broad-based taxing powers. The result is a powerful instrument of social protection that has been amazingly successful in many countries.

As indicated throughout this paper, however, social insurance is not devoid of problems. The problems in developing countries are especially severe, so serious that some people now consider putting much greater emphasis on other alternatives. But as we argue below, the most frequently mentioned alternatives also have major deficiencies.

Other mechanisms

Given the prominent role played by social insurance in this century, most policymakers are very familiar with both its achievements and also areas where it has been deficient or problems have arisen. Often forgotten or less well known to many are the growing problems associated with the major programmes that are complementary to social insurance. Social insurance programmes have never been designed to operate alone, but instead are typically viewed as just one "pillar" of a more elaborate social protection structure.[11] Hence in making informed judgements, it is not sufficient to focus on social insurance programmes alone. *Any reconsideration of the role of social insurance needs to take into account and contrast the historic performance of complementary mechanisms and the concerns that have arisen with regard to their operation.* The four most important "mechanisms" are: (a) the family, (b) social assistance, (c) employer-sponsored pensions, and (d) voluntary or compulsory savings schemes.

The family

In many countries, the nature of the family has changed significantly. First, what we have seen in recent decades is the concurrent phenomena of decreasing family size, rising female participation in the labour force, increased numbers of older people, and rising numbers of the very old (who often require extensive health and social supports). These changes put increasing pressures on the family.

Second, even as the demands on the family increase from "demographic ageing," the family as an institution in society is under significant stress as a result of growing marital instability, increased geographic mobility, limited economic capacity, and changing attitudes about family "obligations."[12] One unfortunate result is that "the development of the urbanization process and the increase of industrial progress lead many people to live in cities in anonymity and loneliness within the nuclear family."[13]

Fortunately, despite all the problems enumerated above, evidence indicates that many families continue to function well, providing economic and social supports to various family members at appropriate times of need. Yet it would be a mistake to view "successful families" as operating in isolation from and without the support of key community and governmental institutions. In fact, over time formal institutions have been given additional responsibilities for

---

11. There are many countries with three so-called pension "pillars": (a) basic statutory schemes, (b) supplemental (especially occupational) schemes, and (c) various individual savings schemes. See, for example, the discussion in Winfried Schmähl, ed. *The Future of Basic and Supplementary Pension Schemes in the European Community – 1992 and Beyond* (Baden-Baden, Germany: Nomos Verlagsgesellshaft, 1991).

12. These issues are elaborated upon in Peter McDonald. "Ageing in Asia: The Role of Families," in *International Symposium on Ageing: Policy Issues and Future Challenges*. Proceedings (Beijing: China National Committee on Aging, 1989), pp. 45-53.

13. Department of International Economics and Social Affairs, Centre for Social Development and Humanitarian Affairs. *The Family: Strengthening the Family – Guidelines for the Design of Relevant Programmes*. No. 4 (New York: United Nations, 1987), p. 9.

assisting families and, in some cases, taking over some of their traditional responsibilities. While this trend can be expected to continue, it is important to view these historical developments as *efforts to supplement and support the family* and its traditional roles — not as a deliberate policy to supplant the family.

Key support from families

Cowgill points out that "the status of older people vis-à-vis their grown children varies widely around the world. This ranges all the way from an authoritarian or domineering relationship toward their children to a complete reversal of role, resulting in abject dependence of the parents on their children."[14] While the nature of the authority and power relationships vary among its members, *families remain a key mechanism for nurturing, for distributing (and redistributing) economic resources, for dealing with and protecting family members from a variety of economic insecurities (disability, widowhood, unemployment, etc.) and for the provision of basic shelter and the dominant living environment.*[15] As Kendig, et al. observe, "family ties can provide the base for redistributing substantial amounts of resources in line with the needs and capabilities of the generations as they pass through the life cycle."[16] In short, the family has been, and remains, critical in the provision of support when people become old and threatened by economic deprivation, disability, and social isolation.

Many examples and statistics could be given to show the extent of family supports provided to the aged in both developed and developing countries. Cattell, to cite only one of many possible examples, reports on the situation in rural Kenya, basing her findings on interviews carried out over the 1983-1987 period.[17] Cattell's data for 200 women and 216 men indicate that 92 per cent of the women and 88 per cent of the men received help from at least one child. This assistance included — in order of importance — non-money gifts of various

14. Donald O. Cowgill. *Aging Around the World* (Belmont, CA: Wadsworth, 1986), p. 83.

15. For a more exhaustive list of family functions (including many non-economic functions), see D. J. Mangen, V. L. Bengtson, and P. H. Landry Jr., eds. *Measurement of Intergenerational Relations* (Beverly Hills, CA: Sage, 1988).

16. Hal L. Kendig, Akiko Hashimoto and Larry C. Coppard, eds. *Family Support for the Elderly: The International Experience* (Oxford: Oxford University Press for the World Health Organization, 1992).

17. Maria G. Cattell. "Models of Old Age among the Samia of Kenya: Family Support of the Elderly," *Journal of Cross-Cultural Gerontology,* vol. 5 (October 1990): pp. 375-394. See also, Margaret Peil. "Family Help for the Elderly: A Comparative Study on Nigeria, Sierra Leone, and Zimbabwe," *Bold,* vol. 2 (1992): pp. 2-4.

kinds, money, and services (fetching wood and water, preparing food, repairing the house, etc.).

Families remain important

It is a commonly held myth that many families ignore, and often abandon, old people in industrialized countries. One should not be deceived by the fact that large numbers of older people live apart from their children in these countries. As Hashimoto points out, "physical distance (not living together) is not equivalent to emotional distance."[18] The fact is that most families in developed countries continue to remain a very important source of support in old age. Higher per capita income levels and pension programmes (both public and private) in these countries allow greater independent living among the elderly. But when older people become frail and lose some or all of their ability to "provide for themselves," the family usually assumes responsibility for providing needed assistance.

"Research as well as experience continue to affirm that the family [in industrialized countries] is the major provider of [long-term] care for the elderly. Studies [in the United States] have shown that approximately 80 per cent of the elderly, dependent in functional activities of daily living, are receiving care from family members. In Israel this figure reaches 86 per cent in some areas where research has been conducted."[19]

Changes in developing countries?

It is a widely accepted belief that the process of industrialization leads inevitably to the breakdown of the extended family and its replacement by the "modern" nuclear family. However, research on the family in recent years questions this conclusion and indicates that the matter is much more complicated, both historically and in terms of what is happening in developing countries today.[20] The extended family never was the dominant family type in some

---

18. Akiko Hashimoto. "Living Arrangements of the Aged in Seven Developing Countries: A Preliminary Analysis," *Journal of Cross-Cultural Gerontology,* vol. 6 (1991), p. 359.

19. Brenda Morginstin. "Impact of Demographic and Socio-economic Factors on the Changing Needs for Services for the Very Old," in International Social Security Association. *The Social Protection of the Frail Elderly.* Studies and Research No. 28 (Geneva: International Social Security Association, 1990), p. 13.

20. J. Hajnal. "European Marriage Pattern in Perspective," in D. V. Glass and D. E. C. Eversley, eds. *Population in History* (London: E. Arnold, 1965); E. Anthony Wrigley. "Reflections on the History of the Family," *Daedalus* (Spring 1977): pp. 71-85; Sandeep Chawla. "The

countries, and in some countries where it is, it does not appear to be diminishing in any significant way — even in the face of industrialization and modernization. In still other countries, changes are indeed occurring, with "the extended family as a traditional household unit ... generally disintegrating in the face of modernization, industrialization, and urbanization, leaving the practice of extended living mostly in rural areas of these countries."[21] For example, a recent popular media review of the situation in India asserted: "a silent revolution, a coup of sorts, is taking place. The patriarch, the matriarch, the eldest son, the aging boss, and the village elder are being elbowed aside. The youth are moving in. Children are even throwing their parents out."[22]

Given the complexity of evolving family structures in various countries, a great deal of caution is required in stating what the family can and should do in support of the elderly. As pointed out by Kendig et al., policy discussions today are all too frequently "based on unsubstantiated generalizations about the supposed abandonment of the aged by families in industrial countries, or of older people being left behind by rapid social change in developing countries."[23] Again, the reality is much more complex in both types of countries.

What is perhaps most clear is that the pressures created by the promotion of economic growth, together with the severe resource constraints confronting developing countries, encourage countries to put heavy emphasis on families in dealing with the insecurity and diminished capacity often arising in old age.[24] But as Chawla observes, the family is expected to deal with the challenges of

Participation of the Elderly in Development." Paper prepared for the Expert Group Meeting on Policies and Strategies for the Participation of the Elderly in Development (Malta: reproduced, February 1988); Nana Araba Apt. "The Role of the Family in the Care of the Elderly in Developing Countries," in R. L. Kane, J. G. Evans and D. Macfadyen, eds. *Improving the Health of Older People: A World View* (Oxford: Oxford University Press for WHO, 1990), pp. 362-380.

21. Op. cit., Apt, 1990, p. 371. For an excellent discussion of the "quiet revolution the demography of intergenerational family life," see V. Bengtson, C. Rosenthaland L. Burton. "Families and Aging: Diversity and Heterogeneity," in Robert H. Binstock and Linda K. George, eds. *Handbook of Aging and the Social Sciences*,3rd ed. (New York: Academic Press, Inc., 1990), pp. 263-287.

22. Madhu Jain and Ramesh Menon. "The Greying of India," *India Today* (September 30, 1991), pp. 46-55 (p. 47).

23. Op. cit., Kendig, et al., 1992, p. 4.

24. See the case studies and discussion in Martin B. Tracy. *Social Policies for the Elderly in the Third World* (Westport, Conn: Greenwood Publishing Group, 1991).

ageing precisely at "the moment when it is under severe and virtually implacable pressures all across the developing world."[25]

The size problem

But there is an even more fundamental limitation to the role that the family can play both before and after industrialization occurs. Although people since earliest times have attempted to mitigate or eliminate economic insecurity by banding together in groups, the approach often does not work. *The major problem with the family (and various other group associations) for sharing is that the number of people involved is often relatively small.* As Kenneth Boulding has observed, "it is when the 'sharing group' becomes too small to ensure that there will always be enough producers in it to support the unproductive that devices for insurance become necessary. When the 'sharing group' is small there is always a danger that sheer accident will bring the proportion of earners to nonearners to a level at which the group cannot function."[26] History retells over and over again the inability of families to deal with the recurrent social welfare problems arising from regional food shortages, pestilence, forced migration, war, rampant inflation, recessions and depressions, ethnic conflicts, political instability, and so forth.

How should governments react to this dilemma? Many policymakers in developing countries fear that increases in general government assistance to older people will cause families to reduce (maybe stop) their help. But there is the strong evidence (as cited above) from the experience of industrialized countries to date that *government and employer-sponsored programmes for the elderly have not generally diminished in any significant way the willingness of families to provide economic and social support to older members of the family who are in need.* What has changed in these countries is the ability of older people to maintain economic independence into old age, largely as a result of economic growth and the concurrent development of collective social protection networks, especially social security.

Fortunately, "who should support the elderly?" is not an either-or question. Government programmes are rarely designed to completely replace traditional kinds of protection. Local communities and occupational groups often develop fairly sophisticated social protection schemes for their members.[27] Clearly there

---

25. Op. cit, Chawla, 1988, p. 16.

26. Kenneth Boulding. *Principles of Economic Policy* (New York: Basic Books, 1958), p. 236.

27. Ehtisham Ahmad. *Protecting the Vulnerable: Social Safety Nets and Public Policy*, IMF paper (Washington, DC: Fiscal Affairs, International Monetary Fund, 1991); Ehtisham Ahmad.

is no need to choose between, on the one hand, supporting or relying on the family and, on the other hand, government action. *A combination of self and family support, local community assistance, and government action can be complementary and desirable.* Of course, the *mix* varies "widely from one society to another due to such things as economic conditions, political and social structure, and traditions."[28]

If we accept the proposition (stated above) that expansion of government policies and collective programmes (public and private) can effectively supplement and support families in their traditional roles *without substantially supplanting them*, then government action becomes not only appropriate but a necessity. "Thus, the question is not one of who should give more support — state *or* family. It is rather a matter of finding the appropriate mixture of support systems".[29]

The historic development of public and private pensions in the West is a long story that will not be discussed at this point in the paper. There are many reasons why pensions were created to supplement traditional family protection. One of those reasons is *the clear preference of individuals in various countries to remove a major part of the "economic support in old age obligation" from the family domain. Not only are families seriously limited in what they can do (as discussed above), but many individuals in the various countries clearly preferred to provide for their own old-age and not be obligated (and subservient) to their own children.* Economic growth and the pension mechanism provide the opportunity to achieve that desire. And it is not surprising, therefore, to find very early in the history of various nation-states political support among the people for *collective income programmes* (both public and private) that promised to achieve that objective. Moreover, it is clear that this political support is even stronger today and is not limited to industrialized countries.[30] The result has been a clear

---

"Social Security and the Poor: Choices for Developing Countries," *The World Bank Research Observer,* vol. 6 (June 1991): pp. 105-127.

28. Op. cit., Kendig et al., 1992, pp. 10-11.

29. Op. cit., Hashimoto, 1991, p. 379.

30. Over the past decade, there has been increased questioning of the collective approach, especially regarding social security programmes in Europe and North America. The questioning has involved considerable debate in the political arena. However, public support has remained very strong and no major changes in the existing programmes have occurred. See, for example, International Social Security Association. *Conjugating Public and Private — The Case of Pensions* (Geneva: International Social Security Association, 1987); Theodore Marmor and J. Mashaw, eds. *Social Security: Beyond the Rhetoric of Crisis* (Princeton, NJ: Princeton University Press, 1988); Sally R. Sherman. "Public Attitudes Toward Social Security," *Social Security Bulletin,* vol. 52 (December 1989): pp. 22-16.

change in the extent to which families are relied upon for economic protection in old age. And we see no strong evidence that similar preferences for self-help and economic independence do not exist in developing countries today.

Social assistance

Families are not the only protection mechanism whose role has *decreased* in many countries. Without doubt the most important 20th century change that has occurred in the matter of old age economic support has been the shift in many countries from, first, reliance on the family and, second, reliance on social assistance schemes. The move to a much greater reliance on pensions has indeed been significant.

While the history of pension development varies greatly among industrialized countries, *one common and important pattern has emerged in most countries: a shift away from means tested "welfare benefits" going to the poor aged in favour of pension programmes providing income replacement benefits for a broad spectrum of the population.* In developing countries, of course, the shift has been much less. In these countries, the development of pensions is still typically at an early stage of evolution. Consequently, the family remains the principal source of support, and a variety of social assistance programmes continue to play an important role.

In fact, over the past decade there has been a renewed interest in many countries (both developed and developing) with regard to shifting towards *greater* reliance on means-tested programmes.[31] Given relatively low economic growth and, in many countries, rising pension costs and projections of significant demographic ageing — policymakers in these countries have begun to think again about the possible advantages (such as lower costs) of targeting benefits through means-testing. For example, economist Gary Becker recently wrote, "sooner or later budgetary deficits and tax burdens will force ... countries to do what has been until now politically unthinkable — to replace Social Security systems in their present form with systems of benefits only for the needy elderly."[32]

The reasons for the earlier shift towards pension and away from social assistance programmes in both developed and developing countries are many

---

31. Taxation of benefits should not be confused with traditional means-testing. In some countries there is now more interest in taxing pension income which heretofore had little or no tax liability on it (typically for individuals with high *total* income).

32. Gary S. Becker. "Social Security Should Benefit Only the Elderly Poor," *Business Week* (January 16, 1989): p. 20.

and complex.[33] The continuing debate over the two approaches for social protection contrasts the advantages and disadvantages of programmes that restrict benefits to smaller numbers of people versus programmes that are universal (or aspire to universalism).

A major argument made for the universal approach is political. Supporters feel that an adequate response to the needs of lower income groups depends on programmes that help *all* income groups. As Wilbur Cohen has argued, in discussing social protection programmes in the United States:

> ... a program that deals with the poor will end up being a poor program. There is every evidence that this is true. Ever since the Elizabethan Poor Law of 1601 [in Great Britain], programs only for the poor have been lousy, no good, poor programs. And a program that is only for the poor — one that has nothing in it for the middle income and the upper income — is, in the long run, a program the American public won't support. This is why I think we must try to find a way to link the interests of all classes in these programs.[34]

Historically, selective programmes have proven to be individually stigmatizing, socially divisive, and politically vulnerable in most countries.[35] Universal programmes, in contrast, are seen by their proponents as generating widespread political support and as promoting social cohesion and national solidarity. This broad economic and political base provides the potential for them to be *effective* anti-poverty programmes.[36] As Peter Baldwin observes with regard to the historical developments in Europe, "if all were included, with burdens spread far and fairly, no one could be abandoned as hopeless, no one could be too fortunate to escape a share."[37]

Another major argument made for universal programmes relates to the universal nature of many problems. Problems of old age support, disability, and

---

33. See, for example, John Myles. *Old Age in the Welfare State: The Political Economy of Public Pensions* (Boston: Little, Brown, 1984); P. Flora and A. J. Heidenheimer, eds. *The Development of Welfare States in Europe and America* (New Brunswick, NJ: Transaction Books, 1981); Irwin Garfinkel, ed. *Income-Tested Transfer Programmes: The Case For and Against* (New York:Academic Press, 1982); and Gosta Esping-Andersen. *The Three Worlds of Welfare Capitalism* (Princeton, NJ: Princeton University Press, 1990).

34. Wilbur J. Cohen and Milton Friedman. *Social Security: Universal or Selective?* Rational Debate Seminars (Washington, DC: American Enterprise Institute, 1972).

35. Theodore Skocpol. "Sustainable Social Policy:Fighting Poverty Without Poverty Programs," *The American Prospect,* vol. 1 (2): pp. 58-70.

36. Robert B. Hudson and Eric R. Kingson. "Inclusive and Fair:The Case for Universality in Social Programs," *Generations* (Summer/Fall 1991): pp. 51-56.

37. Peter Baldwin. *The Politics of Social Solidarity* (Cambridge: Cambridge University Press, 1990), p. 51.

unemployment, for example, are not problems that just confront low income people. They are problems that cut across the broad spectrum of society — supporting the notion that universal programmes may be appropriate.

In contrast, many advocates of targeted social assistance programmes fear that universal programmes will promote the growth of government and the growing dependence of individuals on government — both representing, in their opinion, a threat to economic growth and political freedom. Moreover, advocates of means-testing argue that by targeting benefits, one can ensure a better reallocation of income while minimizing the distortionary effects of the taxation necessary to pay for the benefits.[38] Not only will a selective programme be more "target efficient," say the advocates, it is likely that more support will be available to those most in need, since available resources will be divided among a smaller number of people. Of course, as we just pointed out, those supporting universal programmes strongly disagree, seeing the total resources available for these purposes as much more dependent on general political support (with very little political support going historically to programmes benefiting only "poor people").

But opposition to social assistance does not rest on politics alone. There has been (and still is) widespread dissatisfaction with the functioning of past (and current) means-tested programmes. Major problems are high administrative costs, imprecise targeting (i.e., including or excluding the wrong people because of the typical complexities of rules and procedures), the stigma related to receiving benefits, the abuse of power by those determining eligibility,[39] and the consequent low participation rates by those eligible. The result has been widespread hostility to this approach by large numbers of both citizens and policymakers alike. This hostility has been heightened further by both the resulting disincentives to participation and the incentives for cheating that typically arise.

Finally, many people point to the economic incentive issues associated with social assistance programmes.[40] Benefits must be deliberately kept inadequate;

---

38. Sheldon Danziger, R. Haverman, and R. Plotnick. "How Income Transfer Programs Affect Work, Savings, and the Income Distribution: A Critical Review," *Journal of Economic Literature*, vol. 19 (September 1981): pp. 975-1028.

39. For example, programme officials in some developing countries normally expect some payment from applicants (i.e., a bribe payment before approving eligibility requests — making it impossible for the most impoverished (who have no money) to obtain benefits.

40. There is a similar but probably more controversial discussion over the labour and savings disincentive effects of social insurance retirement pension programmes. See Henry J Aaron. *Economic Effects of Social Security* (Washington, DC: The Brookings Institution, 1982).

otherwise there will be strong incentive for people not to work, to work less, or to work in the underground (often illegal) economy.[41] In the Anglo-American nations, for example, the 19th century was the era of the "poorhouse welfare state."[42] The main problem at the birth of industrial capitalism was inducing people to become "workers" — to make their labour available for sale in "markets" on a regular basis. One way of encouraging people to enter the labour market was to abolish traditional forms of social assistance ("outdoor relief") and to make community support in times of need conditional on entry into a poorhouse where living conditions were deliberately made almost intolerable. The poorhouse, as Charles Dickens described in a number of his famous novels, did its job in this manner quite effectively!

A more contemporary example is means testing in rural China. Family support has been supplemented by a system of basic guarantees *(wu bao)* for those destitute and without aid from kin. As observed by Ahmad, "the emphasis has been more on preventing the 'nondeserving' from getting relief, rather than ensuring that all the deserving are covered. Thus, there is severe social stigma attached to *wu bao,* which restricts take-up rates... The consequence has been an ineffective rural safety net that will take time to reform."[43]

Even when benefits are very low, evidence exists that social assistance programmes sometimes "trap people in poverty" as a result of the work disincentives created by the implicit high marginal tax rates resulting from the various rules related to programme eligibility. Moreover, these programmes typically negate any incentive to save, since programme eligibility is usually dependent on participants keeping savings below some minimal amount.

To be sure, both universal and means-tested programmes currently exist in all industrialized countries and in most developing countries. The difference among countries remains primarily one of emphasis. But if social assistance is to play a greater and more effective role in the future, better solutions must be found to the political, administrative, and economic problems that arise.

---

41. See, for example, Martin Feldstein. "Should Social Security Benefits Be Means Tested?" *Journal of Political Economy*, vol. 95 (June 1987): pp. 468-484 and op. cit. Garfinkel, 1982.

42. D. Rothman. *The Discovery of the Asylum* (Boston, MA: Little, Brown, 1971).

43. Ehtisham Ahmad. *Poverty, Inequality, and Public Policy in Transition Economies*. Paper prepared for 47th Congress of the International Institute of Public Finance (Washington, DC: reproduced, 1991), p. 9.

Employer-sponsored pensions

Until recently, employer-sponsored pensions in developing countries have mostly been special government plans covering civil servants, military personnel, and certain workers in large public sector corporations and various financial institutions. However, although data are fragmentary, there are indications that there are numerous private plans operating in some countries, especially where there are multinational corporations. In Mexico, for example, Vittas and Skully report that there are over 2,000 private plans of various types (some quite minimal in their provisions).[44] Coverage estimates are subject to wide error; data indicate, however, that 2 to 4 million people are covered by these plans.

Employer-sponsored pensions, both public and private, exist in all industrialized countries. Until recently they have played a relatively insignificant role in old age income provision. But in the last two decades their importance has grown rapidly in a number of industrialized countries. The first workers to receive such pensions in most countries have been those working for governments — military personnel and civil servants. Over the years, however, pensions sponsored by private employers have risen in importance. In some countries (e.g., Canada, the Netherlands, Switzerland, and the United States) private pensions constitute a major source of retirement income. And in others (e.g., Australia and Japan) income from these plans is currently small but growing rapidly.[45]

Employer-sponsored plans in the private sector go by different names in different countries: private pensions, occupational pensions, complementary plans, private superannuation, corporate or company plans, supplementary plans, or employee benefit plans. The names and terminology associated with plan implementation procedures also vary greatly. And the approaches and mechanisms for ultimately providing benefits to individuals vary even more.

---

44. Dimitri Vittas and Michael Skully. *Overview of Contractual Savings Institutions*. Working Papers, Country Economics Department, WPS 605 (Washington, DC: World Bank, March 1991). The 4 million coverage estimate given by Vittas and Skully is controversial. Giovanni Tamburi (former social security chief for the ILO), in private conversations with the author, estimated that not more than 2 million are covered (based on his review of the Mexican data).

45. The literature on the origins of employer-sponsored pensions around the world is very sparse. For a brief overview and references, see James H. Schulz and John Myles. "Old Age Pensions: A Comparative Perspective," in Robert H. Binstock and Linda K. George, eds. *Handbook of Aging and the Social Sciences*, 3rd edition (New York: Academic Press, 1990), pp. 398-414.

While plan characteristics governing payments to eligible workers vary widely, it is important to mention two general approaches whose relative advantages and disadvantages have been the subject of considerable debate in many countries: "defined benefit" versus "defined contribution" plans. Defined benefit plans promise a specific benefit based on various formulas, which typically reflect years of service and often take into account earnings.[46] In defined contribution plans, the level of, or process of determining, periodic contributions into a worker's pension account are predetermined, and therefore the ultimate amount of benefits received varies with both contributions and the investment return on the worker's accumulated funds. The controversy centers around (a) the differences in approach of each type of plan with regard to total costs, (b) the different burdens of the regulatory environment on providers, (c) how well the plans respond to the financial priorities of younger versus older workers, (d) who assumes the risks of inflation related to investment experience, and (e) differences in ease and cost of administration.[47]

Another major difference among plans relates to pension pay-out procedures. In some countries (for example, Australia and Japan), most employer-sponsored retirement benefits are paid out in one lump sum payment or in a series of payments over a relatively short period of time. In other countries, benefits are paid out as annuities over the life-time of the worker (and often of a surviving spouse). Critics argue that the lump sum approach encourages workers to use the pension money for non-retirement purposes and increases the likelihood of financial distress in old age. Many countries, therefore, discourage lump sum payouts through tax policies.

With regard to the structure and financing of employer-sponsored pension benefits, three approaches stand out. In some countries (for example, Finland and Germany), employers set up "book reserve plans" that do not actually accumulate pension reserve funds. Instead pension obligations to future pensioners are recorded on the company's records, and benefits are paid out of current operating funds. In contrast, in most countries a legally separate pension fund or foundation is set up and reserves are created to meet accrued financial obligations to meet future benefit payouts. A variant of the funded approach (especially in the United States and Canada) is for employer-sponsored plans

---

46. Many defined benefit plans also take into account the amount of social insurance pensions to which a worker is entitled, "integrating" the two plans in either an implicit or explicit way.

47. Excellent summaries of this debate are found in Employee Benefit Research Institute. *Economic Survival In Retirement: Which Pension Is for You?* (Washington, DC: The Institute, 1982) and Zvi Bodie. "Pensions as Retirement Income," *Journal of Economic Literature*, vol. 28 (March 1990): pp. 28-49.

to be set up and administered by insurance companies, typically operating under special laws regulating that industry.

Closely related to the financing structure of employer-sponsored plans is the extent to which governments seek to guarantee that promised benefits will actually be received by workers (and their families). Many countries have regulatory statutes and supervisory organizations that set funding and fiduciary standards and also monitor various aspects of the pension administration activities carried out by employers or unions (or their representatives). Some countries go further. For example, in Germany and the United States special agencies have been created to provide formal benefit guarantees to potential pension recipients threatened by the termination of private pensions with inadequate financing (the Pensions-Sicherungs-Verein in Germany and the Pension Benefit Guaranty Corporation in the United States).

Advocates of employer-sponsored plans make the following major arguments in their favour:

- Unlike social insurance, which because of its broad coverage must remain very uniform in its programme provisions, employer-sponsored pensions can be more flexible and can be tailored to meet differing situations and conditions of various industries, particular firms, or different occupational groups. This flexibility can be used to design plans that can stress both employers' goals for managing their labour force and any special retirement needs that workers have.[48]

- Employer-sponsored pensions are seen as an effective way to increase national savings, promote investment, and thereby facilitate economic growth.

- Given the inadequacy of and/or possible equity and financing problems associated with government pension programmes, employer-sponsored plans are viewed by some policymakers as a feasible and desirable alternative.[49]

All these arguments are highly controversial. With regard to the first, flexibility, the historical evidence indicates that while different plans serve the

---

48. For example, employer-sponsored pensions have been used by management to encourage the workers they do not value highly to leave the company or retire early.

49. A recent summary and evaluation of the literature critiquing public social protection approaches is provided in Alain Euzéby and Jef van Langendonck. *Neoliberalism and Social Protections: The Question of Privatisation in the EEC Countries* (Geneva: International Labour Office, 1990).

different needs and preferences of various groups of workers, *most of the key design characteristics of plans have been dominated by the economic interests of the employers that sponsor them.*[50] Over the years, many employers have used their pension plans (a) to promote greater efficiency in the productive process by facilitating the hiring and departure of those workers perceived to be the most/least productive, (b) to promote the retention of workers (especially white-collar professionals), (c) to help in adjusting the company's workforce to shifting demand, and (d) to manipulate the pension plan funding process to contribute both to the firm's special financial needs and to the profitability situation management wishes to convey in its financial statements. As discussed below, *these management objectives often conflict with the retirement provision interests of the workers in the plans.*

With regard to the question of the extent to which funded pensions (either private or public) contribute to saving, investment, and economic growth, there is no consensus of opinion among economists on the matter and only highly controversial empirical evidence on the link between pensions and higher growth. There is a common misconception among non-economists that there is a direct relationship between saving (by individuals and businesses) and economic growth. In fact, while there is a need for saving to facilitate investment in any economy, there are a variety of ways saving can be accumulated, and there is no guarantee that a rising savings rate will necessarily increase productive investment and, through this investment, economic growth.[51]

With regard to the third argument listed above, the extent to which employer-sponsored pensions should be substituted for public plans depends not only on the problems related to, say, social insurance (discussed below) but on the problems related to employer-sponsored plans. The experience in many countries has shown that very serious problems arise in connection with employer-sponsored plans:[52]

---

50. William Graebner. *A History of Retirement* (New Haven, CT: Yale University Press, 1980); L. Hannah. *Inventing Retirement – The Development of Occupational Pensions in Britain* (London: Cambridge University Press, 1986); Jill Quadagno. *The Transformation of Old Age Security: Class and Politics in the American Welfare State* (Chicago, IL: University of Chicago Press, 1988).

51. See, for example, Henry Aaron. *Economic Effects of Social Security* (Washington, DC: The Brookings Institution, 1982); Selig D. Lesnoy and Dean R. Leimer. "Social Security and Private Saving: Theory and Historical Evidence," in Charles W. Meyer, ed. *Social Security: A Critique of Radical Reform Proposals* (Lexington, MA: Lexington Books, 1987), pp. 69-101; Franco Modigliani. "The Key to Saving Is Growth, Not Thrift," *Challenge*, vol. 30 (May-June 1987): pp. 24-29; Alan J. Auerbach and Laurence J. Kotlikoff. "Demographics, Fiscal Policy and US Saving in the 1980s and Beyond," in Lawrence H. Summers. *Tax Policy and the Economy*, vol. 4 (Cambridge, MA: MIT Press, 1990).

- Coverage: unless coverage is mandated by government, large proportions of the labour force are generally left uncovered by employer-sponsored plans or are covered by plans that impose high-risks on workers and/or inadequate benefits. Often uncovered are those people who are most vulnerable economically and most in need of supplementation to provide basic protection.

- Vesting and portability: in the absence of government legislated standards, employers typically have set up plans that serve primarily their own objectives in managing the labour force — denying pensions to many job-changers, job-losers, and sometimes (to save money) to workers with very long tenures who "do not make it" to eligibility status; the result has been constraints on labour mobility, serious horizontal inequity, and inadequate (or no) benefits for many worker who expected and counted on receiving benefits.

- Survivors' benefits: there is great variation in the extent to which benefits are made available to the survivors of workers; moreover, the provisions of plans often encourage workers to gamble on surviving their spouse — resulting in inadequate retirement income for female survivors when the male worker (typically) dies before her.

- Early retirement provisions: eligibility and benefit provisions are often used by employers to force or encourage workers to leave the company, biasing the retirement decision, shrinking the labour force (since most do not take new jobs), and threatening the long-term viability of retirement incomes that are subject to inflation over a longer period of time.

- Funding: problems of both over- and underfunding have arisen because of the great uncertainty associated with key forecasting variables (such as price and wage changes, the turnover of labour, and interest rate levels) and disagreement over the appropriate discount rate to be used.

- Lost benefits: many worker benefits have been totally lost or reduced significantly as a result of (a) plans being inadequately funded when companies go out of business, (b) poor investment practices resulting in low or negative returns on reserves, and/or (c) the misappropriation or embezzlement of pension funds.

- Disclosure problems: although plans are complex and vary greatly from employer to employer, there is often little effort put into providing workers with the information necessary to assess these plans and the role they are likely to play in providing income in their particular retirement situation;

---

52. These issues are discussed in more detail in James H. Schulz. *The Economics of Aging*, 5th edition (NY: Auburn House, 1992).

thus, it is not uncommon to find large numbers of workers with unrealistic expectations relating to their plan, followed by surprise and anger when they do not actually get the benefits they expected or thought were promised.

- Inflation: in the absence of indexed securities or government guarantees, employer-sponsored plans cannot fully protect workers' pensions from inflation after retirement occurs; the result is (a) that benefits paid *at the time of retirement* may suffer inflation erosion, and (b) vested benefits and benefits paid out *during* retirement are almost certain to be eroded — the seriousness being a function of the time period involved and the inflation rate.[53]

- Maturation: when first established, it takes individual plans 30 to 40 years to "mature." This makes it difficult to provide workers close to retirement with adequate pensions. Often companies setting up "defined benefit plans" will give older workers "past service credits" for pre-plan years with the company, which helps to solve this problem. This action, however, typically creates very large unfunded pension liabilities; the result is higher risks of lost benefits if the plan terminates. The maturation problem is much more difficult to solve for "defined contribution plans," accounting historically (in part) for the popularity in many countries of defined benefit plans during the early years of employer-sponsored plan development.

Various governments have reacted to these problems by legislating a variety of mandated pension provisions and standards (e.g., reduced years of employment required for vesting), setting up supervisory and regulatory agencies to control abuse, and establishing government mechanisms that guarantee workers minimum benefits (in the face of, inflation or plan termination).[54] These efforts have not come cheaply — resulting in much higher administrative costs for employers and substantial budgetary costs for the governments.[55] Large government bureaucracies are created, and vast amounts of regulatory repor-

---

53. In practice, many plans use formulas that base benefits on recent earnings, which often provides a large degree of inflation adjustment. In contrast, very few plans index benefits during retirement; some adjust benefits on an *ad hoc* basis, but typically these adjustments fall far short of the inflation rate.

54. See, for example, Zvi Bodie and Robert C. Merton. "Pension Benefit Guarantees in the United States: A Functional Analysis," in Pension Research Council. *Symposium on the Future of Pension in the United States*, Compendium of Conference Papers (PA: Pension Research Council, 1992).

55. A recent study in the United States documents the rapidly growing, and now very high, administrative costs associated with defined benefit plans. See Hay-Huggins Company. *Pension Plan Expense Study for the Pension Benefit Guaranty Corp.* (NY: Hay-Huggins, 1990).

ting and statistical information need to be processed. And with government regulation have come higher employer costs to meet both the legislated standards and the reporting requirements of the regulatory authorities. The result is often the increased reluctance of employers without plans to start one.[56] As a result, it seems doubtful whether (for this and other reasons) the large segment of the labour force not covered by these plans will ever be covered without mandating by government. As pointed out by Holzmann, "international evidence suggests that, unless mandated, massive tax preferences are required to induce the establishment of complementary schemes on a large scale."[57]

Voluntary and compulsory savings plans

Unlike employer-sponsored pensions, savings plans give more emphasis to personal initiative through individualized personal saving. Various types of arrangements have been developed that enable individuals to put money into special accounts to be used only for specified contingencies, a major one being retirement. Usually these plans are encouraged by special tax rules, usually tax deferrals, that give substantial financial advantages to individuals saving money in this way. Often the accumulations in these special accounts cannot be withdrawn, without substantial penalties, until a person reaches a specified age. Some of these plans are voluntary, while others are compulsory.

Looking first at voluntary plans, some countries (e.g., the United Kingdom and the United States) have had for many years special tax laws that allow *self-employed* individuals to establish savings plans that receive special tax preferences. A more recent development in various countries is the creation of special saving opportunities for *salary and wage workers* meeting various eligibility criteria (such as lack of employer-sponsored pension plan coverage). For example, in Canada the self-employed, workers not covered by employer plans, and workers with "low" employer plan coverage can set up "registered retirement savings plans (RRSPs).[58]

---

56. Pension Research Council. *Symposium on the Future of Pensions in the United States*, Conference Papers (PA:Pension Research Council, 1992). One of the major themes of this conference (and its papers) was the adverse effects of increased government regulation and the "pension guarantee insurance" programme currently operating for defined benefit plans in the United States.

57. Robert Holzmann. "The Provision of Complementary Pensions: Objectives, Forms and Constraints," in *International Social Security Review*, vol. 44 (1-2/91): pp. 75-93 (p. 89).

58. Monies in these RRSPs can be withdrawn in the form of (a) a life annuity (with options available for a guarantee period and/or survivor payments), (b) an annuity-certain (i.e., payments do not depend on one's continual survivorship) payable to age 90, or (c) a special

Certain workers and their spouses in the United States can set up "individual retirement accounts" (IRAs). The IRA legislation in the United States permits individuals who are not "active participants" in an employer-sponsored plan (and certain other individuals meeting specified eligibility conditions) to contribute a maximum sum yearly into accounts administered by various kinds of financial institutions (banks, brokerage houses, insurance companies, mutual fund companies, etc.). Income taxes on the contributions and their earnings are deferred until paid out of these special accounts.[59] The law permits individuals to roll over account balances from one IRA to another. Most "early distributions" (prior to age 59½) are subject to a 10 per cent penalty tax.

In some cases, voluntary savings plans are *set up by employers*. In the United States, for example, federal tax laws encourage employers to set up savings plans for their employees. While some of these plans are "profit sharing" or voluntary employee contribution plans with no employer contribution, most are plans where the employer *matches* some proportion of the worker's contribution.[60]

While these voluntary schemes provide greater freedom of choice, they are subject to a number of problems. As pointed out by Vittas and Skully, "their ability to meet the retirement needs of savers depends on the solvency and investment performance of the institutions with which they are entrusted" and are subject to "much higher operating and marketing expenses, especially if no restrictions are placed on the ability of individual members to transfer their pension accounts."[61] The willingness and ability of individuals to invest "wisely" is complicated by (a) the myopic behavior of many individuals that tends to encourage undersaving, (b) the complexities of financial investment in general, (c) the often confusing and sometimes misleading information put out by the money managers trying to attract more business, and (d) the risks of inflation, especially given the fact that indexed securities are not usually available.[62]

---

payout scheme ("registered retirement income fund") that allows unlimited variability in the amounts withdrawn, subject to a minimum amount each year after age 71 and total withdrawal by age 90.

59. Individuals with "adjusted gross income" above specified levels can make the same contributions into IRAs, but tax deferment is less than 100 per cent on their contributions. However, taxes are deferred until payout on all the earnings arising from these contributions.

60. Currently, to qualify for special tax treatment, annual contributions per participant cannot exceed 15 per cent of compensation, or US$30,000 − whichever is less. The maximum contribution rate is typically 5-6 per cent of earnings.

61. Op. cit., Vittas and Skully, 1991, p. 47.

62. On the matter of the difficulty of retirement planning for the individual, see James H. Schulz, op. cit., 1992. With regard to myopic behavior, see Laurence J. Kotlikoff. "Justifying Public

However, perhaps the strongest criticism made against this approach is a matter of equity. Voluntary programmes, supported by government "tax expenditures,"[63] are utilized disproportionately by higher income individuals.[64] In the United States, some studies indicate that not only are these plans used disproportionately by high income people, they also do *not* increase personal savings (as advocates claim). Rather, it is argued, they have merely caused a shifting of assets, resulting in substantial tax revenue loss.[65]

With regard to *compulsory* plans, there are both publicly and privately administered plans. *Government administered* savings plans called provident funds exist in a number of developing countries.[66] Normally both employers and workers are required to make regular contributions (typically a per cent of earnings) into special worker accounts, which are administered or supervised by government agencies.

The payouts are usually in a lump sum and are paid out (a) upon reaching a designated age (most commonly 55 for men; 50 for women), (b) *before* reaching

Provision of Social Security," *Journal of Policy Analysis and Management,* vol. 6 (1987): pp. 674-689.

63. The term "tax expenditures" refers to the special provisions in the tax law that reduce the amount of tax revenues that would normally be available to the government under the more general provisions of the tax law. The expenditures contrast with regular government expenditures of money on goods, services, or transfers. Voluntary savings schemes typically permit individuals to defer until taken out at retirement (or at other times) any tax payments on the income put into these plans.

64. For United States data illustrating this issue, see John R. Woods. "Pension Coverage Among Private Wage and Salary Workers: Preliminary Findings from the 1988 Survey of Employee Benefits," *Social Security Bulletin,* vol. 52 (1989): pp. 2-19. For Canadian data see Robert L. Brown. *Economic Security in an Aging Population* (Toronto:Butterworths, 1991), Chapter 6.

65. Empirical studies in the United States have reached differing conclusions, resulting in continued controversy over the issue. For a review of various studies, see Jonathan Skinner. "Individual Retirement Accounts:A Review of the Evidence,"*Tax Notes* (January 13, 1992): pp. 201-212.

66. For example, Fiji, Gambia, Ghana, India, Indonesia, Kenya, Kiribati, Malaysia, Nepal, Nigeria, Papua New Guinea, Singapore, Solomon Islands, Sri Lanka, Swaziland, Tanzania, Vanuatu, Uganda, Western Samoa and Zambia. For a detailed discussion of provident funds see John Dixon. "Provident Funds in the Third World: A Cross National Review," *Public Administration and Development,* vol. 2 (1982): pp. 325-44 and John Dixon. "Provident Funds: An Assessment of their Social Security, Social, and Economic Performances and Prospects," in James H. Schulz and Deborah Davis-Friedmann. *Aging China: Family, Economic, and Government Policies in Transition* (Washington, DC: 1987), pp. 173-93.

the designated age to meet special designated needs (such as major illness or buying a home), or (c) upon disability or death of the worker.

As with other defined contribution schemes, the adequacy of provident fund benefits depends on a long contribution period. During the early years of such plans (i.e., the "startup period"), the maximum possible contribution period for older workers is insufficient to allow such workers to accumulate sizeable accounts. Also, in the past and currently, the capacity of provident funds to provide significant economic support in old-age has been constrained: (a) by the relatively low level of contributions in some countries, (b) by special pay-outs from the accounts before old-age, (c) by an inability to ensure that lump sum payments are used to provide long-term, old-age protection, and (d) by very low interest rates (sometimes below the inflation rate) paid by the governments managing the funds. With regard to the last concern, Vittas and Skully observe:

> National provident funds are often established as paternalistic institutions and may be subject to considerable political interference. They have the potential to accumulate substantial reserves, which can then be used to fund the government debt, to support "high capacity" sectors or activities or to acquire stakes in private industry. But if the reserves are not invested wisely, or if contribution are low, the final benefits may be inadequate to meet the retirement needs of members. In national provident funds, the [income] replacement, investment and inflation risks are borne by employees. The solvency and integrity of the funds depends on their real rate of return and their administrative efficiency.[67]

More recently, compulsory savings plans *administered by the private sector* have been instituted in the United Kingdom and Chile. Starting in July 1988, employees in the United Kingdom were permitted to contract out of the government run "State Earnings Related Pension Scheme" (SERPS) or (since employers are permitted to contract out of the SERPS) to contract out of the employer-sponsored pension. To do this, it is compulsory that individuals set up a personal pension plan in one of four ways: (a) the purchase of an insurance policy or annuity contract, (b) the establishment of a unit trust, (c) the deposit of money into a bank, or (d) the deposit into what are called "building societies" or "friendly societies". To encourage employees to contract out, the British government has offered generous rebates of past contributions to the state scheme, an explicit earnings-related subsidy, and an option to revert to the state scheme.

While experience with the "personal pension" in the United Kingdom is limited, some serious problems have already arisen, generating considerable debate. The Life Assurance and Unit Trust Regulatory Organisation (LAU-

---

67. Op. cit., Vittas and Skully, 1991, p. 8.

TRO) "reports an increasing number of cases in which inexperienced or un-scrupulous insurance salesmen are arranging transfers that are detrimental to the client's interests and serve only to line the salesmen's pockets."[68] Given the complexity of pensions and the government regulations related to them, most individuals do not understand how to analyze the options and hence do not know the implications of transferring out of occupational schemes into personal pensions. According to LAUTRO, many financial advisers and salesmen give little or no attention to helping individuals compare alternatives – instead pushing the personal pension option where they receive at least four per cent commission (often more) on the transfers.

An entirely different issue arises from the monetary incentives introduced by the government in 1986, to encourage people to leave SERPS. In early 1991, the Comptroller and Auditor General reported that the total costs of these incentives had reached £9.3 billion (eight times the original forecast). But the popularity of the incentives, instituted to make future government SERP financial payments more manageable by reducing the number of people in the programme, seems to have made the financial situation worse. Estimates now indicate that net future costs are likely to be around £6 billion higher.[69] Critics argue that the result is a huge bonanza for insurance companies (through fees and commissions) and a large, inequitable misallocation of government money that does little to help the lower and middle class in old age.

A great deal of attention has been given in recent years to the compulsory savings plan that was established in Chile during the early 1980s.[70] All wage and salary workers are required to participate (except for the military and workers employed before the plan began who choose to remain covered under a prior social insurance programme). Employers are required to put 10 per cent of each worker's wage or salary into a privately administered retirement fund; the worker chooses from among those investment companies that are officially approved and regulated by the government. Participants are also permitted to make voluntary contributions up to a specified maximum.

The funds that each Chilean worker contributes are kept in a separate account (in an "indexed currency") and can easily be moved from one retire-

68. Debbie Harrison. "Bad Buys in the Transfer Market," *Financial Times* (February 29, 1992): p. 43.

69. David Hencke. "Pensions Opt-out Cost Soars," *Guardian* (January 3, 1991).

70. "The Chilean experience shows that a bold reform of a bankrupt public pension system is feasible, despite the presence of several complex issues that inhibit similar initiatives in other countries." (p. 35)[Dimitri Vittas and A. Iglesias. *The Rationale and Performance of Personal Pension Plans in Chile*, World Bank Paper (Washington, DC: reproduced, 1992)]

ment fund to another at the discretion of the worker. At retirement the worker can choose to receive a price-indexed life annuity based on the accumulated funds or can opt to make "scheduled withdrawals" from the fund (choosing, if they wish, to start up an annuity at a later date).

While there is a very large element of private sector involvement in the Chilean scheme, it is important to understand that *in reality the Chilean programme is as much a public scheme as it is a private one*. The government-approved private sector companies administer the funds and market their administrative/investment expertise (to take away business from competitors and attract funds from workers). However, the Chilean government assumes major responsibility for much of what goes on in the plan and has committed itself to pay large sums of money to finance the scheme.[71] At the current time, the government is responsible for:

- setting capitalization requirements for investment firms and approving their participation in the programme;

- overseeing the transition and providing funding credits for workers who shifted from the old social insurance plan to the new scheme;

- guaranteeing to all workers a "minimum pension";

- acting as a payor of last resort to ensure a minimum real rate of return (relative to the average returns of all funds) on monies invested with any particular investment company[72];

- determining what types of investments may be purchased by the investment companies and the maximum amounts of any particular type of investment that can be held in portfolios;

---

71. The government financial commitments arise in four basic areas: (a) prior-service credits ("recognition bonds" or *bonos*) provided to allow and encourage workers to shift from the old social insurance programmes to the new system; (b) a high minimum old-age benefit for those covered for at least 20 years; (c) the costs of a large bureaucracy to supervise and regulate the private companies; (d) the potential costs of the other guarantees described in the list of government responsibilities. Based on a recent visit to Chile, actuary Robert J Myers comments, for example: "Mammoth amounts of general revenues are currently required for the new system, and will be required for many years to come. "See, Robert J. Myers. "Privatizing Social Security: It's Not Exactly One Size Fits All," *Contingencies* (November/December 1991): pp. 9-11.

72. Investment firms are required to provide accounts with a real investment return that is no less than half the average paid by all pension investment firms. If the firm cannot meet this profitability requirement out of its investment returns and/or its investment reserves, the government is obligated to make up the difference.

- controlling and supervising investment firm operations and investment decisions — based on detailed reports on investment transactions, the fund's financial accounts, and the processing of monies coming into and going out of the fund;

- supervising the separate, and different, disability and survivor benefits programmes, which are financed by additional worker contributions to the investment companies but administered primarily by insurance companies; and

- guaranteeing old-age annuity payments, as well as disability and survivor benefits, in the event that any insurance company fails.

There has been a great deal of controversy outside Chile on the merits of the Chilean plan.[73] The success of the Chilean scheme in the years to come depends not only on the private firms competing with one another but on the quality of supervision by the government regulators and the ability and willingness of the government to meet its many financial responsibilities under the compulsory savings programme. Thus, it will be many years before we have sufficient historical experience to definitively compare this approach with other mechanisms.

The origins of social insurance

Up to now, ageing issues have *not* been a major concern of most leaders in developing nations of the world for at least four major reasons. First, preindustrial societies are predominantly *rural* societies: where the economic and political position of older persons relative to younger persons is generally strong; where families, by both structure and necessity, are supportive of needs in old age; where older people are able to remain economically productive for a greater portion of their lifetime; and where much of the population is outside of wage-dependent markets. Second, the aged are a relatively small proportion of the total populations of such nations (given relatively low life expectancies and high fertility rates). Third, governmental development priorities favour expenditures that invest in the long-term productive potential of the young. And fourth, the elderly are often viewed (probably incorrectly) as impeding development because they are more resistant to change and are less adaptive "human capital."

---

73. For a positive view see op. cit., Vittas and Iglesias, 1992; for a more guarded view see Colin Gillion, "The Privatisation of Pension Schemes in Latin America: The Chilean Model." An ILO paper (Geneva: reproduced, 1992).

Rising interest in pensions

Paradoxically, while governments in developing countries, until now, have shown little interest in "the aged," there has been a great deal of interest in pensions.[74] As in the industrialized West, social insurance pensions in developing countries were preceded by pensions for military and civilian officials employed by governments. Pensions in many of these countries, however, have also been influenced in a major way by pension schemes designed to cater largely to the needs of expatriate workers in the urban areas of various colonies before independence. With the needs of expatriates in mind, provident funds were established in many colonies, impeding the subsequent development of social insurance programmes in most of the nation states that followed independence.[75]

A second development in the colonies was the creation of mutual benefit societies. These societies now exist in countries as diverse as Algeria, India, the Ivory Coast, Malaysia, Nigeria, the Philippines, Senegal, Singapore, Tanzania, and Zaire. Mutual benefit societies were modeled after the European "friendly societies" in, for example, France, Belgium, and Great Britain. Over the years, some of these mutual benefit societies (especially in Latin America) have evolved into or have been replaced by pensions.[76]

Social insurance pension schemes have now been legislated by governments in many developing countries. A wide variety of factors have influenced their adoption — ranging from simple imitation of "Western practices" to new efforts designed to deal with the growing economic insecurity among the elderly resulting from industrialization and international market fluctuations. Perhaps most important, the *traditional* sources of economic insecurity confronting individuals and families (which we discussed earlier) have not diminished as these countries progress — creating continuing demands for effective social protection programmes.

---

74. J. Midgley. *Social Security, Inequality, and the Third World* (Chichester, UK: Wiley, 1984). Midgley provides a review of some social security developments occurring throughout the Third World. See also the discussion by James H. Schulz. *The World Ageing Situation 1991* (United Nations Office at Vienna, 1991, op. cit.).

75. K. Thompson. "Trends and Problems of Social Security in Developing Countries in Asia," in International Labour Office, Regional Office for Asia. *Social Security and National Development* (Bangkok: ILO, 1978), pp. 50-56.

76. Op. cit., Mesa-Lago, 1985.

The rationale for collective action

As we discuss in more detail below, many serious issues have been raised in connection with the social insurance programmes in developing countries. There are major questions related to coverage, financing, the adequacy of benefits (especially given inflation), distributional equity, and possible adverse effects on the economic development process itself.

Before addressing these issues and possible future action that might be considered, it is appropriate at this point in the discussion to review why the "mechanism" of social insurance is so widely used throughout the world to deal with the economic security needs of older people. While much of the debate over pensions focuses on the relative advantages of public versus private pensions, there are two more basic questions that we need to be clear about. Why is there a need for *any kind* of pension programme, and should individuals be compelled (either by the government or an employer) to join a particular pension programme?

At the very beginning of this paper we listed a variety of historic developments and work-threatening problems that can adversely effect the economic security of people as they grow old. The so-called "retirement" period of life can be a welcomed life event or a time to be feared; in large part it depends on the extent of an individual'scontrol over the timing of the retirement *decision* and also on his or her economic situation during the retirement period. A number of major problems confront any individual trying to make economic preparations for retirement on their own:

- One doesn't know with certainty when he or she (or their spouse) will die.

- One doesn't know exactly what the future preretirement income flow (e.g., earnings) will be, given the fact that work opportunities are ever changing, health/disability problems often arise, and (for women) child-raising interruptions may occur.

- One doesn't know what ones basic retirement needs will be (especially the costs related to "long-term care") nor what life-style will be ultimately preferred for that period.

- One doesn't know the age of retirement, given changing employment policies, discrimination against older workers, and unpredictable health.

- One cannot easily predict the future rate of inflation, which depreciates the value of those assets put aside for retirement that do not adjust fully.

- One cannot predict with great accuracy the rate of future economic growth — growth that is likely to affect one's attitudes about retirement aspirations and one's economic position in retirement relative to the working population.

The number and nature of the problems listed above indicate that individual retirement planning is a very difficult job. Thus, faced with all this uncertainty, many individuals (economists call them the "risk-averse") welcome collective mechanisms that reduce the risk at reasonable cost.[77]

But risk reduction in reaction to the above list of problems is not the only reason for collective action. Individual behaviour and market failure are also important explanations. Economic modeling typically makes assumptions that decisions are rational and that the information necessary to make these decisions is widely disseminated and used; a large amount of economic, historical, and psychological evidence raises important doubts about these assumptions.[78] Historical experience indicates, for example, that financial preparation for retirement is often inadequate because of "myopia [i.e., short-sighted saving behaviour], misinformation, miscalculation, and simple laziness."[79] Given that the personal decision-making process involved in preparation for retirement is so complex, many find it beyond their capacities to cope with the issues; some try to ignore them; and others try to cope but fail.

Thus, Pechman, Aaron, and Taussig argue that this reality describes a situation where individuals are willing to give up some of their freedom of choice and control over financial decision-making — being willing to delegate decision-making on these matters to others (especially experts) and join together in collective action. They conclude:

> There is widespread myopia with respect to retirement needs. Empirical evidence shows that most people fail to save enough to prevent catastrophic drops in post-retirement income ...Not only do people fail to plan ahead carefully for retirement, even in the later years of their working life, many remain unaware of impending retirement needs ....In an urban, industrial society, government intervention in the saving-consumption

---

77. What is "reasonable"? A risk-averse individual, in theory, will buy insurance as long as its net cost does not exceed the value (to the buyer) of the greater certainty provided by such insurance.

78. See, for example, Henry J. Aaron and Lawrence H. Thompson. "Social Security and the Economists," in Edward D. Berkowitz, ed. *Social Security After Fifty* (NY: Greenwood Press, 1987), pp. 79-99 and Daniel Kahnneman and Amos Tversky. "Judgement Under Uncertainty," in Peter A. Diamond and M. Rothschild, eds. *Uncertainty in Economics* (NY: Academic Press, 1978).

79. Laurence J. Kotlikoff. "Justifying Public Provision of Social Security," *Journal of Policy Analysis and Management*, vol. 6 (1987): pp. 674-689. See, also, Peter A. Diamond. "A Framework for Social Security Analysis," *Journal of Public Economics*, vol. 8 (1977): pp. 275-298.

decision is needed to implement personal preferences over the life cycle. There is nothing inconsistent in the decision to undertake through the political process [we would say: through a private or public collective process] a course of action which would not be undertaken individually through the marketplace.[80]

Security in large numbers

How does insurance reduce risk? The first problem listed above is that the individual does not know exactly when he or she will die — that is, how long a period to provide for. This means that any person (or family) preparing for retirement must assume the "worst" — a long life — and put aside enough money to take care of that eventuality; or one must be prepared to rely on private or public charity if one lives "too long" and one's own economic support is exhausted.

A pension programme provides an attractive option by utilizing a basic insurance principle. If the number of individuals in a pension programme is sufficiently large, mortality tables of life expectancy can be constructed that show estimates of average life expectancy at particular ages. Retirement preparation costs can then be geared to *average* life expectancy, with the "excess" payments of individuals who die before the average age going to those who live beyond it. The result is that no one has to pay more than they would need to put aside personally if it was known with certainty that they would live for a period of years equal to the average life expectancy.

The second problem is the lack of predictability regarding future income. For example, chronically low earnings, ill health, or periods of unemployment may make sufficient saving for retirement very difficult or even impossible. Also, health or employment problems may force an individual to leave the labour force unexpectedly, often much earlier than was originally planned. As pointed out by Drèze and Sen, "the time pattern of earnings may not at all match the time patterns of needs. Indeed, sometimes the needs are maximal precisely when incomes tend to be minimal (for example, when a person is seriously ill)....[and private] capital markets and insurance markets are frequently non-existent or feeble (especially in developing countries)."[81]

80. Joseph A. Pechman, Henry J. Aaron, and Michael K Taussig. *Social Security: Perspectives for Reform* (Washington, DC: The Brookings Institution, 1968), pp. 61-62.

81. Jean Drèze and Amartya Sen. "Public Action for Social Security: Foundations and Strategy," in Ehtisham Ahmad, Jean Drèze, John Hills, and Amartya Sen, eds. *Social Security in Developing Countries* (Oxford: Clarendon Press, 1991), pp. 1-40.

Collective arrangements to deal with this problem are not new. As we pointed out earlier, people since earliest times have attempted to mitigate or eliminate economic insecurity by banding together in groups — families, tribes, associations, or guilds. And in many countries — particularly those less industrialized — the family still remains the major source of economic protection and security in old age.

The major problem with the family (and many other group associations) for sharing risk is that the number of people involved is relatively small and therefore that their numbers can be overwhelmed by events (sickness, crop failure, depression, inflation, etc.). *Thus, the need for better collective arrangements to deal with the economic problems of old age has always been with us.*

Why compulsory pensions?

Action to respond to the myopic behavior of individuals (i.e., their lack of foresight and their poor planning) is often referred to as the *paternalistic* rationale for compulsory pensions. However, it can be argued that compulsion is also appropriate from both an *altruistic* and a *self-interested* point of view. Kenneth Boulding concisely states the principal argument:

> [If an individual] were rationally motivated, [he] would be aware of the evils that might beset him, and would insure against them. It is argued, however, that many people are not so motivated, and that hardly anyone is completely motivated by these rational considerations, and that therefore under a purely voluntary system some will insure and some will not. This means, however, that those who do not insure will have to be supported anyway — perhaps at lower levels and in humiliating and respect-destroying ways — when they are in the nonproductive phase of life, but that they will escape the burden of paying premiums when they are in the productive phase. In fairness to those who insure voluntarily, and in order to maintain the self-respect of those who would not otherwise insure, insurance should be compulsory.[82]

Laurence Kotlikoff expresses the argument in yet another way:

> Suppose each person in society is altruistic and cares about the welfare of all other individuals. While each individual may be altruistic towards everyone else, those who fare better economically will end up transferring resources to those who fare poorly. Since each individual can anticipate such transfers in the event of bad luck, each individual will have an incentive to free ride on the generosity of others in considering how much to save.[83]

In addition to the costs imposed on the families or taxpayers who must provide the support, there are costs on society as a whole. Malnourished people

---

82. Op. cit., Boulding, 1958.

83. Op. cit., Kotlikoff, 1989.

living on inadequate income can contribute little, if anything, to the production process and may even impose costs on the general population through crime and other social disruptions.

Another but very different argument for compulsion is a more pragmatic financial one. In the United States, for example, the architects of the social security old age insurance programme argued that a programme with optional coverage would make it actuarially difficult to project with sufficient accuracy both benefits (costs) and revenue. It was feared that this problem would create financial instability and make it difficult to guarantee adequate and equitable benefits as social security developed.[84] The decision of the United States to have a compulsory pension programme is in no way unique. There are few countries in the world with a social security old age pension programme that has designed a large amount of voluntary coverage into the programme. In Japan and the United Kingdom, workers must participate in a basic social insurance plan that provides a flat-rate benefit, but employers (and, in turn, individual workers) can opt out of a second-tier earnings-related national pension, if the employer (or worker) provides at least equivalent coverage through private means. Like the United States, many countries have special public pension programmes for special groups of workers (especially government employees), and many exclude from coverage certain groups (such as farm workers, the self-employed, or employees of very small firms). Some countries — for example, Ghana, Germany, Kuwait, Liberia, Peru, Uganda, and Zambia — have voluntary coverage, but these noncompulsory provisions *are all limited* to certain (usually small) groups in the country.

If we shift our attention from public pensions to *employer-sponsored* pensions, we find that the situation is not very different. Most of the workers who are covered (or not covered) by these plans have *not* achieved that status by personal election. Not all firms have established plans for their employees, but almost all employer-sponsored pension schemes that have been set up are compulsory. Typically, once a worker joins a firm, he or she automatically becomes a member of the pension plan — sometimes after a waiting period. There are some employer-sponsored plans, however, that provide for an employee contribution out of salary; such plans sometimes make coverage optional.

In summary, we see that the usefulness of pensions in helping to provide for economic security in old age is generally accepted and that compulsory coverage remains a feature of both public and private programmes.

---

84. J. Douglas Brown. *An American Philosophy of Social Security* (Princeton, NJ: Princeton University Press, 1972).

How appropriate for developing countries?

While public pension are found throughout the developing world, there is still the need to be clear about why they exist. Could it be that the social insurance schemes in developing countries are inappropriately based upon the conceptual and organization structures designed for the historical and cultural circumstances of industrialized countries in the West?[85] Our answer to this question is "mostly no."

The rationales for collective action that were presented in the paragraphs above are clearly applicable to developing countries. The risks associated with growing old exist *in all countries* — as does the complexity of the tasks associated with economic preparation for retirement. In fact, the risks and planning complexities are probably even greater in developing countries where the incidence of general health problems, disability, premature death, and unemployment (to name a few of the risks) are less predictable. Also, "a related market problem in developing countries is a lack of markets for many types of risk" and the fact that the financial institutions for safely "storing" financial wealth for old age are not as well established.[86] Where the institutions exist, there are typically more risks associated with them — including employer-sponsored pension plans, the major alternative to public pensions.

On the other hand, history and cultures do vary from country to country. What "works" in one country may not work or be as acceptable in another. These differences are not just between the West and the South. There is, in fact, great variation among industrialized countries in their approaches to providing economic support in old age. Esping-Andersen documents that the composition and mix of public and private sources of income are not independent of one another in industrialized countries.[87] Instead, they reflect fundamental differences in the types of "welfare state" regimes found in various market-oriented democracies.

Esping-Andersen distinguishes between three *regime* types in industrialized countries. The first is what he calls the *social democratic* approach, found mainly in the Scandinavian countries; it rests on universal principles of solidarity among citizens, provides high wage replacement across the entire labour mar-

---

85. See a section entitled "Disadvantages to Industrial Country Models" in op. cit., Tracy, 1991, which discusses the "absence of prerequisites," declining confidence, and cultural divergence that discourage developing countries from accepting with enthusiasm the Western approach.

86. Op. Cit., McGreevey, 1990.

87. Op. cit., Esping-Andersen, 1990.

another in industrialized countries.[87] Instead, they reflect fundamental differences in the types of "welfare state" regimes found in various market-oriented democracies.

Esping-Andersen distinguishes between three *regime* types in industrialized countries. The first is what he calls the *social democratic* approach, found mainly in the Scandinavian countries; it rests on universal principles of solidarity among citizens, provides high wage replacement across the entire labour market through public programmes, and incorporates those without labor market entitlements into labour-market based programmes. In contrast, there are the *liberal*, market-oriented regimes found in the Anglo-American democracies; here there is a tendency towards greater reliance on means- or income-tested social assistance and a strong emphasis on "private" occupational benefits (subsidized by government). A final type is the *corporatist* or status-based welfare state found in various continental European economies (e.g., Austria, France, Germany, and Italy); the approach in these countries reflects less social democratic concern with citizenship and less liberal concern with market efficiency, emphasizing instead the maintenance of a traditional social order and the preservation of status differentials across class and occupational boundaries.

The "Welfare State"

Before looking in more detail at the current situation in developing countries, a brief review of the developments in the industrialized countries will provide useful historical insights. The various approaches to support for the elderly in the West have also varied and evolved over time. Initially, public old age pensions were designed as benefits for the poor. They were social assistance (by another name) "for the elderly" — who were for the most part indigent, unable to support themselves, and increasingly unable to get adequate support from their children. This *social assistance welfare state* provided low, subsistence level benefits.[88] Unlike the welfare state that followed, the purpose of these pensions in most countries was *not* to allow ageing workers to *retire*, i.e., to withdraw from the labour market in advance of physiological decline. Rather,

---

87. Op. cit., Esping-Andersen, 1990.

88. The "welfare state" concept is very ambiguous, being defined in different ways by various writers. Here we use the term to refer to the large-scale creation of government social policies and programmes with broad coverage to supplement private mechanisms. Controversy arises with regard to what "large-scale" means; some would call Sweden a welfare state but not the United States. Our view is that all industrialized countries have assumed such broad responsibility for social welfare policies that they can all be called welfare states.

the first plans focused on providing survival benefits, if and when old age took its toll on earnings capacity in the labour market.

After World War II, very different public pension programmes began to develop. At this point, the *social security welfare state* appears. It was based on two key principles of state distribution: universality and wage replacement.[89] Universality meant less targeting of benefits to the "poor" and extending the boundaries of the welfare state to include a growing "middle class" of high wage workers. Wage replacement meant that benefits now had to be sufficient, not merely to prevent poverty but also to provide "income security" (i.e., to maintain continuity in living standards between the pre- and post-retirement years for a labour force accustomed to a high standard of living).

The transition from heavy reliance on "social assistance" to an emphasis on "social security" did not occur overnight. It took a variety of forms in different countries, in part reflecting national differences in the design of the programmes already in place. However, while each country developed its unique approach, there was also simultaneously the development of international standards that sought to influence and guide the policymaking in the various countries. In 1944, for example, the "Declaration of Philadelphia" committed the International Labour Organization (ILO) to furthering "the extension of social security measures to provide a basic income to all in need of such protection and comprehensive medical care" [Section III(f)]. In the years that followed, the ILO adopted numerous conventions and recommendations designed to guide countries in their development of social protection policies.

Prior to World War II, social assistance to the elderly was provided in several ways. A common form was the old age pension found in countries like New Zealand (1898), Australia (1908), the United Kingdom (1908), and Canada (1927), where eligibility for small benefits was based on a means-test. After World War II, primary reliance on means-tested programmes ended in most countries, and universal benefits programmes became very popular. The latter programmes were distinguished by the fact that there was no linkage between benefit levels and previous contributions or earnings. These *flat-benefit* programmes operated in many countries — including Britain, Canada, the Netherlands, and Sweden.

---

89. See James H. Schulz, G. Carrin, H. Krupp, M. Peschke, E. Sclar, and J. Van Steenberge. *Providing Adequate Retirement Income: Pension Reform in the United States and Abroad* (Hanover, NH: University Press of New England, for Brandeis University Press, 1974); John Myles. *Old Age in the Welfare State: The Political Economy of Public Pensions* (Boston, MA: Little Brown, 1984).

Universality, however, did not bring real income security (i.e., continuity of living standards after retirement), since the benefits provided remained low. To deal with this problem, some countries added a second, earnings-related pension on top of a flat-benefit. Sweden led the way in this direction, introducing a two-tiered system in 1959. The Canadian and British parliaments passed laws introducing similar systems in 1965 and 1978, respectively.

The transition from an emphasis on social assistance to relying primarily on social security in other countries (e.g., Germany, France, Italy, Austria, and the United States) was different, reflecting the fact that in these countries *from the beginning old age benefits were related to past earnings and contributions*. While benefits in the early years were at subsistence levels and the extent of coverage varied in these countries, the earnings-related structure facilitated the later transition to the social security welfare state. The change usually occurred as a series of incremental reforms — additions to an already existing structure — without the need for radical new legislation.

For example, West Germany began debating social security reform almost immediately after the Second World War was over. In Germany, a broad political spectrum of parties and voters agreed that there was a major role for the state in social policy. Therefore, given the existing pension structure, it was relatively easy to achieve consensus on reform. This consensus included agreement on raising pensions to replace about 60 per cent of preretirement income and introduced pension indexation, adjusting pensions for both real growth and inflation. The new pension legislation was enacted in 1957. The law dramatically changed public pensions in Germany and was studied by other countries considering major changes.

In the United States, *coverage* under social security expanded to most of the labour force through a series of amendments between 1950 and 1965. *Income replacement* levels were raised in a series of changes between 1968 and 1972 to levels that approximated "income security" standards. Though incremental in appearance, the American results were almost as dramatic as the changes in countries where major restructuring of programmes took place. Thus, after the social security amendments of 1972, Robert Ball, then head of the U.S. Social Security Administration, observed that the United States had "a new social security system."[90]

The German and American experiences were not atypical, however. The transition to the social security welfare state took place in virtually all Western

---

90. Martha Derthick. *Policymaking for Social Security* (Washington, DC: The Brookings Institution, 1979), p. 339.

countries through a series of reforms culminating in the late sixties and early seventies.

Does history repeat itself?

How unique is the historical development of the welfare state in the West with regard to public pensions? As we stated above, there was great variation among the various countries themselves (and still is). And certainly with regard to social welfare, many things are different today among developing countries. We must not lose sight, however, of some very important commonalities that are extremely relevant to developing countries today. As development takes place, every country must deal with the fact that the nation state's activities "are interlocked with the market's and the family's role in social provision." [91] That is, in addition to the reasons for collective action discussed above, there are other factors that arise out of the development process itself.

We have already pointed out that industrialization puts strains on family support mechanisms. But industrialization also changes the basic nature of work and creates new ways for people to achieve income:

> Workers become dependent on a money wage and leave behind the former means of subsistence and support within the village or tribe. When the wage is interrupted, through sickness or accident, old age or invalidity, the means of livelihood disappears. In the early stages after the transition from the country to the town, the victims of "social accidents" may look to the traditional protection of the extended family and the village community, but the ties quickly weaken. [92]

The shift of people away from farming and other self-employment occupations complements the rise in "labour markets." Increasing numbers of people can no longer directly exchange their labour or other assets for things to eat, to wear, and so forth. Instead, individuals must enter labour markets, offer their energies and intelligence for money, and exchange that money for the goods and services they need. Thus, as Cockburn points out in the above quote, a great potential for economic insecurity is created as development proceeds.

Without other resources, people become "vulnerable to coercion when jobs are scarce and insecure to the degree that jobs may become scarce." [93] "With no recourse to property, and no state to which human needs can be directed, the

---

91. Op. cit., Esping-Andersen, 1990, p. 21.

92. Christine Cockburn. "The Role of Social Security In Development," *International Social Security Review,* vol. 33 (1980): pp. 337-358, (p. 343).

93. Charles E. Lindblom. *Politics and Markets: The World's Political-Economic Systems* (New York, NY: Basic Books, 1977), p. 48.

market becomes to the worker a prison within which it is imperative to behave as a commodity in order to survive."[94] However, unlike pots, pans, or TVs, the supply of people is not determined by their saleability in the market. People are not produced or destroyed simply on the basis of their expected value in the market, and some people (e.g., the sick and disabled) have little or no labour power to sell. Moreover, as industrial development continues, the labour of some groups, such as the elderly, is often viewed as no longer having great value.[95] Accordingly, as Polanyi observed and Marx predicted, to allow income distribution to be shaped by markets alone — to organize society as though labour were produced for sale in the market — would probably result in the self-annihilation of society.[96] *Very simply, all economic systems relying heavily on markets need ways of providing for those who cannot participate in markets; labour markets need welfare states, or people will die or revolt (or do both).*

But it is not only the landless person in the labour market who is at risk. Today, more than ever, political systems are embracing the incentive-control mechanisms of "markets" and, in the process, exposing *all their citizens* to the economic insecurity that goes with them. To name but a few examples of what is happening, we see growing international market interdependence among countries, the rising popularity of "privatization", and the establishment of new and expanded "free trade" zones in Europe and between Canada, Mexico, and the United States. Competitive markets — reacting to technological change, shifts in consumer preferences, new sources of productive inputs, and so forth — threaten both workers' jobs and firms' profits if the demands of new economic production possibilities and output "needs" are ignored. With market incentives that promote efficiency, innovation, and growth also come unemployment, inequality, bankruptcy, community decay, and social disruption. James Fallows has expressed it well: "Capitalism is one of the world's more disruptive forces. It can call [through market forces] every social arrangement into question, make cities and skills and ranks merely temporary. To buy into it is to make a commitment to permanent revolution that few political creeds can match."[97] *No developing country that seeks to harness the market mechanism to the "engine of economic growth" can ignore the social problems that are created in its wake.*[98] *It is in this sense that history must repeat itself.*

---

94. Op. cit., Esping-Andersen, 1990, p. 36.

95. See the discussion on this point in op. cit., Graebner, 1980 and op. cit., Myles, 1984.

96. K. Polanyi. *The Great Transformation* (Boston, MA: Beacon Press, 1944).

97. James Fallows. "America's Changing Economic Landscape," *Atlantic Monthly* (March 1985): pp. 47-68, (p. 62).

98. For a discussion of the major role played by social insurance systems in dealing with cyclical

Developing countries will need to create their own special version of the "welfare state." This almost certainly must include new forms of protection for people when they grow older.[99] But the extent to which reliance is placed on the family, community, employers, government, or self-help may be different from what exists today in the West and (as in the West) is likely to evolve over time.

Finally, developing countries cannot ignore another important implication arising out of economic growth itself. Up till now the discussion in this section of the paper has emphasized the fact that social insurance is one of the important responses to certain market failures, various political issues, and a great deal of economic insecurity associated with development. But there is also a very *positive* reason for public and private pensions. As the experience of the West has shown, industrial growth — fueled by rapid technological change — can result in vast increases in economic output. This economic growth provides an expanding opportunity for greater leisure with a simultaneous increase in living standards. In the West, this rapid growth during the 20th century made it possible to support more easily older people who could not or did not wish to work. The increases in leisure experienced early in the century came primarily in the form of shortened workweeks and longer vacations; in contrast, *much of the new leisure in recent decades has been allocated to the end of the lifespan.*[100] A vast amount of research indicates that most older workers in the West want to retire as soon as financially possible, and that once retired, adjust well to their new situation in society, enjoying their increased leisure.[101] The "right to retire" (or what some call "the institutionalization of retirement") is generally viewed as one of the positive contributions of industrialization. In pre-industrial societies there is usually little choice but to work until one is physically unable; there is no retirement role. But, as observed by Friedman and Orbach, another reason pension programmes were developed was to provide "compensation

---

fluctuations in various industrialized countries see, James H. Schulz. "Epilogue: The 'Buffer Years': Market Incentives and Evolving Retirement Policies," in John Myles and Jill Quadagno. *States, Labor Markets, and the Future of Old-Age Policy* (Philadelphia, PA: Temple University Press, 1991), pp. 295-308.

99. See the discussion of options, for example, in Ehtisham Ahmad. "Social Security and the Poor: Choices for Developing Countries," *The World Bank Research Observer,* vol. 6 (June 1991): pp. 105-127.

100. See Chapter 5 in op. cit., Schulz, Borowski, and Crown, 1991. See also Martin Kohli, M. Rein, A. Guillemard, and H. van Gunsteren, eds. *Time for Retirement: Comparative Studies of Early Exit from the Labor Force* (Cambridge: Cambridge University Press, 1991).

101. See op. cit., Schulz, 1992; Robert Atchley. *The Sociology of Retirement* (New York: Wiley Schenkman, 1976); and op. cit., Myles and Quadagno, 1991.

based upon years of service rather than upon need per se. They were to emerge as an 'earned right' and were to become instrumental in defining a retirement status as appropriate for the older worker."[102]

Developing countries today: The reality and the challenge

In recent years social insurance programmes in developing countries have come under sharp attack. For example, an influential publication on "Social security in Latin America," written by economist William McGreevey, comments:

> In addressing [various social risks] ... through social insurance, governments every-where confront moral hazard − the fact that public benefits once proffered will be taken up by those who may not need them − greatly inflating the costs of protecting against the risks themselves. In a broader political setting, benefits once proffered come to be regarded as entitlements and hence no longer subject to review even if they fail to serve the objective for which they were created. With the passage of decades ... the needs of the populations have evolved and the problems of the poor, especially in rural areas, have become more pointed and explicit. The services offered to urban employees through social security seem luxurious by comparison to what governments are able to do for the poorest segments of society.[103]

This provocative statement highlights one major contemporary controversy in *both* developed and developing countries. Today many people ask: are benefits going to people who "don't need them"? As we argued previously, all people (except perhaps the few who are very rich) need group programmes to help overcome the limits and problems of individual/family action. But are the programmes that currently exist the best we can do?

At the beginning of this paper we stated that there is a clear need for nations around the world to reassess their approaches to income maintenance in old age. In developing countries, this need arises not just because of the increasing criticisms coming from international development agencies but also because of changing realities: (a) global ageing, (b) the new international economic environment, (c) growing dissatisfaction with programme operations within countries, and (d) major financial problems.

We organized the discussion to follow into three general categories:

---

102. Eugene A. Friedman and Harold L. Orbach. "Adjustment to Retirement," in Silvano Arieti, ed. *The Foundation of Psychiatry* Vol 1, *American Handbook of Psychiatry*, 2nd ed. (New York, NY: Basic Books, 1974): pp. 609-645.

103. Op. cit., William McGreevey, 1990, p. 1.

- political issues of adequacy and equity;
- management issues of implementation and administration; and
- economic issues.

It is difficult to generalize on these matters. There are tremendous differences in the situations and approaches of developing countries throughout the world. The brief discussion (below) is insufficient to convey the variety of differences and the extent of the complexities.[104] But it does provide the broad outlines for more in-depth discussions and studies related to specific countries.

What benefits? For whom?

As McGreevey (above) and Mesa-Lago (among others) have correctly observed, "political obstacles are perhaps as important as economic ones" in both initially *introducing* and then *reforming* social security programmes throughout the world.[105] Esping-Andersen's recent book examining the evolution of the welfare state in the West makes that point abundantly clear.[106] And as Dréze and Sen similarly observe, "resource constraints should not be overlooked, but it would be a mistake to regard these constraints as the most important obstacle to be overcome in attempts to provide social security through direct public support in developing countries."[107]

A serious political issue arises, for example, as a result of the fact that in many developing countries social insurance coverage is not available to most of the people, is "too generous" for some who get it, and is often inadequate for many of the other recipients. This reality is certainly a reflection of the differences in economic and political power of different groups in each country. But, in no small part, it is also a consequence of historical timing. While the basic idea of social insurance is simple and the tasks of administration relatively minimal, they are "simple" and "minimal" *primarily in comparison to* the much more

---

104. One major difference is the wide variation in work settings. In Rwanda, for example, about 90 per cent of the population lives and works in rural areas, primarily as farmers. In contrast, most of the population in Columbia is urbanized but works in the "informal" sector where work places are not officially registered and where government regulations and laws are rarely enforced.

105. Carmelo Mesa-Lago. *Ascent to Bankruptcy: Financing Social Security in Latin America* (Pittsburgh, PA: University of Pittsburgh Press, 1989) p. 255.

106. Op. cit., Esping-Andersen, 1990. See also John B. Williamson and Fred C. Pampel. *Old-Age Security in Comparative Perspective* (New York: Oxford University Press, forthcoming).

107. Op. cit., Dréze and Sen, 1991, p. 27.

complicated tasks of government (such as national defence) and the implementation and administrative complexities of other social protection programmes
(e.g., education, medical care, and social assistance). Social security programmes in both developed and developing countries — by political and
economic necessity — have evolved over time, changing as new groups have
been included and economic circumstances varied.

In the early stages, social insurance coverage is almost always limited to
urban workers, and *different* programmes are often created to respond to the
needs of *different* groups. Even for these urban workers, however, this coverage
is often restricted initially to only *some* urban workers, given the many financial
and administrative issues that arise. Thus, workers in certain occupations/in-
dustries, in smaller firms, or in certain regions, towns, or cities are often not
covered. The result is a patchwork of different programmes — programmes that
cover *some* groups (but never *all* groups) in the population.

Now, as in earlier periods, when countries stop and reassess the results of
their political histories regarding social insurance development, they often do
not like what they see and think about change. But as Giovanni Tamburi warns
in reaction to the various proposals of foreign advisers for pension reform in
Eastern Europe, in making changes today one cannot assume away the "benefit
culture," obligations, and citizen expectations created in the past.[108] Each
country has a history of providing certain benefits to certain groups, and it is
politically difficult *in any country* to "turn back the clock" and start again. Hence,
reform is almost never easy (to the great irritation of some economists who are
used to assuming away political considerations in their models). Not surprising-
ly, therefore, one finds that a large part of the history regarding social insurance
in various countries is a history of continuous debate over "what benefits and
for whom?"

In assessing the past and debating the future of pension plans, what characteristics or features of the plan should be examined? With an institutional
arrangement as complex as pensions, one can generate a long list of plan
features that might be studied.[109] Opinions differ widely as to which of these are
most important. Moreover, there is little agreement on the relative weights that
should be assigned to each feature when making an overall judgment about a
particular pension plan. Apart from the issue of compulsory versus optional
plans, there are a number of important characteristics of pension plans, how-

---

108. Giovanni Tamburi. "Misunderstanding Pension Privatization — the Case Against Do-It-
    Yourself Pension Kits," *Benefits & Compensation International* (March 1992): pp. 2-8.

109. See op. cit., Vittas and Skully, 1991, pp. 5-7 and op. cit., Schulz, 1992, chapter 4.

ever, that would probably appear on everyone's list of key characteristics. To begin with, pensions should be **available, adequate, fair**, and **understood**. Unfortunately, social insurance programmes in most developing countries today can be criticized with regard to their success in achieving all four goals.[110]

The coverage problem

As we discussed above, social insurance coverage is a major issue.[111] Determining the extent of pension coverage is an often very difficult but important factor in assessing the success of pension plans. Most people would agree that individuals in similar circumstances should not be arbitrarily excluded from coverage under a plan or excluded because of age, sex, race, and so forth.

But as we indicated above, the matter of who is actually included in a pension plan is often complicated by a variety of administrative, technical, political, and economic considerations. For example, in almost all developing countries it has not been possible to cover large numbers of workers in rural areas (where often the majority of the population lives) because of two major difficulties: First, there are very real logistical, technical, and administrative problems in extending coverage to rural areas (problems of registration, communicating with plan participants, compliance, record-keeping, estimating wages or income in agricultural settings, delivering benefits, and so forth).[112] Major, often similar, problems arise when trying to cover workers in the "informal sectors" of the economy.[113]

Probably most difficult are the financial issues: (a) the rural population, most with very low incomes and very little *money* income, finds it difficult to contribute financially to collective schemes;[114] (b) politically it has been difficult to

---

110. This paper focuses on social insurance in developing countries. The statement in the text should not be interpreted to mean that the author does not think there are problems in industrialized countries with regard to these attributes. Certainly problems and debates over these same issues are also frequent in the West.

111. It is also a major problem with regard to employer-sponsored plans.

112. See, for example, International Social Security Association. *Social Security Protection of the Rural Population in Developing Countries* (New Delhi: ISSA Regional Office for Asia and Oceania, 1980). In this connection, it is interesting to note that in the highly industrialized country of the United States in the 1940s, policymakers still found it difficult to extend coverage to farmers, the self-employed, and other groups because of problems associated with collecting the equivalent of "payroll contributions." See Edward D. Berkowitz, ed. *Social Security After Fifty* (NY: Greenwood Press, 1987), p. 20.

113. See, for example, International Labour Office. *Informal Sector in Africa: Jobs and Skills Programmes for Africa* (Geneva: ILO, 1985).

develop redistributive financing schemes (Brazil is one exception) that finance rural benefits from urban revenues; and, (c) "extension of the current system to cover the total population is infeasible in most countries because of the costliness of the current package of benefits."[115] The result in Latin America is that "a minority of the population is covered against all risks, while the majority of the population has no protection at all."[116] Similarly, regarding China, Liu speculates that "the skyrocketing cost of providing social security to state sector employees — a relatively small group of the country's labor force — and its drain on the financial health of enterprises and of the state, is expected to have an adverse impact on the country's national economy."[117]

Thus the current situation in many developing countries might be characterized as growing frustration in the face of an inability to move forward more rapidly to provide social protection to a greater proportion of the country's population. The coverage question has been an issue of concern in most countries for decades and a topic of frequent discussions at international social security meetings.[118] The fact that so little progress can be reported today is an indication of just how difficult the problem is and that there are no ready answers to the dilemma.[119]

Current proposals for reform that may help deal with the lack of collective social protection for large portions of the population include —

Shifting greater responsibility onto other mechanisms:[120]

- increasing government efforts to support and strengthen family support, especially in rural areas; and

---

114. Op. cit., Tracy, 1991, points out, for example, that extension of social security coverage to Mexican farmers in the 1970s had to be rescinded because the farmers had insufficient funds to make the required contributions.

115. Op. cit., McGreevey, 1990, pp. 15-16.

116. Op. cit., Mesa-Lago, 1989, p. 8.

117. Lillian Liu. "Social Security for State-Sector Workers in the People's Republic of China: The Reform Decade and Beyond," *Social Security Bulletin*, vol. 54 (October 1991): pp. 2-16, (p. 11).

118. See, for example, Alfredo Mallet. "Social Protection of the Rural Population," *International Social Security Review*, vol. 33 (1980): pp. 359-393.

119. Similar conclusions were reported over a decade ago (!) to the XXth General Assembly of ISSA in Manila (1980) by Christine Cockburn (see op. cit., Cockburn, 1980).

120. But the reader should take note of our earlier discussions on the limits and problems of alternative mechanisms.

- expanding social assistance programmes that target the poor.

Rethinking and changing the financing approach:

- financing more universal benefits (or better "targeted" programmes) by saving money through actions described below and/or by developing new financing mechanisms to replace or supplement the traditional "payroll tax";

- reducing the costs of current programmes by consolidation of programmes and/or by cutting back on benefits to those currently covered; and

- creating a first tier of "basic benefits" to be extended to all and a second (and perhaps third tier) of supplemental benefits provided through a combination of public/private programmes.

Rethinking the benefits provided:

- "unbundling" the many different benefits and services offered by social security institutes into those that could be extended to the poor and those that are "affordable" only by middle- and upper income groups;

- protecting the rural, and poor population generally, through specialized programmes more appropriate to their situation (e.g., crop insurance programmes and "guaranteed income" programmes); and[121]

- "prioritizing" benefit needs, which are likely to be different in urban and rural areas; giving priority attention in rural areas, for example, to primary and preventive health care, disability protection, and assistance to widows and old persons without access to family support.

The list is long and actually holds out promise.[122] But as we stated at the beginning of this section, the obstacles to reform in this area are more likely to be political than economic. (The technical/administrative obstacles are discussed further below.)

---

121. Examples of programmes that might be studied include the IMSS-Solidaridad in Mexico, peasant insurance in Ecuador, the "indigent" programme of social insurance in Costa Rica, the Agriculture Workers' Pension Scheme in Kerala and the Social Assistance Programme in Maharashtra (India), and the Social Guarantee Programme in Gabon.

122. An excellent review of issues and options on coverage and the other issues discussed here is contained in Carmelo Mesa-Lago. *Social Security and Prospects for Equity in Latin America*, World Bank Discussion Papers, 140 (Washington, DC: The International Bank for Reconstruction and Development/World Bank, 1991).

Adequacy issues

The *existence* of a pension programme and coverage under it is not to be confused with the *level and amounts of benefits actually paid*; in the history of pensions around the world, many plans have existed that paid all too few benefits or "generous" benefits to only a special few.

Moreover, a particular pension plan is often only one of a number of collective programmes operating to provide economic security. It is not sufficient to view a particular pension programme in isolation from these other programmes. For example, eligibility or benefit determination under one programme is sometimes related to benefits received from another programme (i.e., benefits are sometimes "integrated").[123]

Any discussion of a particular pension plan's adequacy must explicitly recognize the variety of means available to the individual (or society) in achieving a particular level of income in old age. Thus, in evaluating the adequacy of any particular pension benefit, it is necessary to relate such analysis to a general framework for evaluating individuals' general economic status and the variety of means available to achieve or change that status. Are individuals expected to accumulate personal savings for their old age? Are all individuals *able* to save for old age? What noncash programmes (such as health insurance) are available to provide economic support? How large are both public and private pension benefits; who is currently covered by each; who should be covered?

There will never be complete agreement about the appropriate roles for the various means of providing income in old age — collective pension schemes are only one major way (see our list of mechanisms beginning on p. 19). Rather, it is almost certain that there will be continuing debate among opposing groups over these matters.

In developing countries, there are two major considerations that are widely raised with regard to the adequacy of benefits. On the one hand, there is concern that the benefits will be too small; on the other hand, there is concern that the benefits will be too generous:

> In countries with high inflation and unindexed benefit formulas or pension payments, the real value of benefits has been eroded by inflation. This has caused a capricious redistribution of benefits from workers with long service and high incomes to those with short service and low incomes.[124]

Also to be considered is the argument that:

---

123. Op. cit., Thomas D. Leavitt and James H. Schulz, 1983.

124. Op. cit., Vittas and Skully, 1991, p. 17.

Social security institutes [in developing countries] will never be able to serve the needs of the poor if they continue to promise 70 per cent or more replacement of wages during retirement and disability.But if the benefits offered by these institutes were reduced to, perhaps, 40 per cent of the basic urban wage, then such benefits could be extended to poverty groups as well as to contributing workers .... Basic income security at a third of the basic wage probably is affordable for all; full replacement of income certainly is not.[125]

Other proposals for changing the benefit structure include:

- eliminating excessive "early retirement" options, raising the normal retire-ment age, and/or making the retirement age for men and women the same;

- providing better, but not necessarily unlimited, protection from inflation;

- incorporating redistributional provisions into programmes (e.g., "a weighted benefit formula" that replaces relatively more preretirement income for lower income individuals than for higher income persons); and

- elimination of seniority pensions that are based on years of service, regard-less of age, and therefore allow retirement at very early ages (e.g., as early as age 40 in Brazil and Uruguay).

Equity

Whether a pension programme is perceived as fair depends in large measure on how the programme treats different individuals and how these individuals think they should be treated. The two issues of coverage and benefit adequacy, as we discussed above, generate a variety of equity issues. Analyses of equity questions tend to focus on financing — how much do the benefits received cost the individual in contrast to other benefit recipients and, possibly, nonreci-pients?

In this regard, an important consideration is the extent to which a pension scheme is designed to redistribute income within the relevant population (to achieve so-called "social adequacy" objectives). In plans that redistribute major amounts of income, there is generally a very weak link between a worker's personal contributions, payroll taxes, and reduced wages (to pay for pensions) and the benefits the worker ultimately receives. Yet the link between pay-in and benefits received is often one major criterion for judging pension equity.

Another issue is the amount of "unintentional redistribution" that occurs in a plan." Unintentional redistribution may result from the effects of inflation on the distribution of benefits within and across generations, but it may also be

---

125. Op. cit., McGreevey, 1990, p. 19.

caused by changes over time in the provisions or performance of different schemes."[126]

Also, redistribution may occur as a result of particular financing arrangements. Concern has been raised by some economists with regard to the redistributional impact of payroll taxes in developing countries. If the uncovered population, many of whom are poor, partially pays for the benefits of the covered population through higher prices of consumer goods, then a serious equity would seem to exist.

Determining "tax incidence" or who ultimately bears the burden of any tax is one of the most complex issues in economics. The result is widespread disagreement among economists on the impact of particular taxes. For example, most economists (based on studies to date) think that the payroll tax *in industrialized countries* is ultimately paid (for the most part) by workers in the form of wages that are lower than what they otherwise would have been. Not all economists in industrialized countries, however, agree with this conclusion.[127] Moreover, McGreevey, reporting on several studies *for developing countries*, warns that much more of the payroll tax may be passed on to consumers in the form of higher taxes in these developing countries.[128]

In addition to action related to the coverage and adequacy issues discussed above, some proposals to making social insurance more equitable include:

- introducing financing methods that offset the "regressiveness" of the payroll tax – such as exemption of wages up to a specified level, a progressive contribution rate structure, or tax credits for certain categories of earners;

- raising or eliminating the payroll tax contribution ceiling that limits the payments of high earners;

- utilizing special taxes to subsidize benefits to low income individuals (e.g., luxury taxes or the Brazilian type of tax on the payroll of urban enterprises and agricultural production); and

- stricter penalties and prosecution of businesses that avoid or delay payroll tax payments.

---

126. Op. cit., Vittas and Skully, 1991, p. 5.

127. Martin S. Feldstein. "The Incidence of the Social Security Payroll Tax: Comment," *American Economic Review,* vol. 42 (September): pp. 735-732; Jane H. Leuthold. "The Incidence of the Payroll Tax in the United States," *Public Finance Quarterly,* vol. 3 (January): pp. 3-13.

128. Op. cit., McGreevey, 1990. But see op. cit., Ahmad. *Protecting the Vulnerable* ..., 1991, for a different view.

Informed participation

It is important that individuals know whether they are covered by a pension plan, what the conditions of entitlement are, what benefits they (or their family) are likely to receive, what the risks of losing benefits are, and various other facts about the plan. Over the years a large amount of evidence has accumulated that indicates that there is a great lack of knowledge and much misinformation among workers in various countries with regard to expected pensions, both public and private. As the number and variety of pension programmes grow and many of these programmes become more complicated, this problem also grows. Therefore, in reviewing existing programmes or proposals for pension changes, the complexity of the programme should be considered. An assessment should be made of the resultant impact on the employees' ability to understand the pension programme and to realistically incorporate its provisions into their pre-retirement planning.

To further these objectives, it has been suggested that:

- governments (and pension organizations) carry out greater educational efforts to explain to people both the strengths and limits of existing programmes; and
- "consolidation" efforts be carried out to minimize the number of programmes and the complexity, inequity, and confusion that can result from a multiplicity of programmes covering (in different ways) a variety of groups.

Implementation and administration

Apart from the benefits paid out by a pension programme, there are a variety of expenditures connected with keeping records, regulatory supervision, determining benefit eligibility, collecting and managing the funds used to pay benefits, and informing individuals of their rights under the plan. In situations where individuals are permitted to choose between different plan managers, marketing costs (including advertising) often become a major expense.

The level of these administrative expenses can significantly influence the amount of benefits an administering authority can ultimately pay out. Thus, Boulding (and others) have argued that one valid criterion for choosing between private and public programmes is whether there can be significant economies of scale in their operation. As summarized by Boulding:

> If there are these economies — that is, if the cost of administering the insurance declines with every increase in the amount of insurance written — then a state monopoly will almost inevitably be cheaper than a number of competing private companies ...We may venture a hypothesis that where the operations of insurance are fairly routine, the

case for state or national monopoly is stronger than where the operations involve great difficulties of definition of rights.[129]

However, even the best designed programme can "fail" if the implementation of that design is faulty. Once programmes are created, organizations of people must be created to run them. Whether we are talking about socialist or capitalist societies (i.e., whether we are emphasizing government or market mechanisms), the major organizations of implementation (government departments, corporations, etc.) are hierarchically structured bureaucracies. While bureaucracies have many positive attributes in their ability to "get the job done," they are far from perfect instruments of policy implementation. The list of problems associated with bureaucracies is well known — rigidity, "red tape," overcentralization, impersonalness, "passing the buck," etc.

Social insurance programmes in developing countries are certainly not free of administrative problems.Before discussing them, however, it is important to emphasize and remind the reader of the obvious. *Problems of so-called administrative inefficiency are ubiquitous — in every country, at every level, in both private and public organizations.* It is always a matter of degree. The differences from country to country and organization to organization can indeed be considerable, however, and do matter!

While one must be cautious about generalizing, there are a variety of problems common to many countries in the developing world.

Skill and training deficiencies

One of the most important problems in social security organizations is the scarcity of high-level, trained personnel.[130] For some countries the problem is especially severe. In Africa, for example:

> The social security schemes set up in the wake of independence were often grafted on to a general administrative apparatus which, given the shortage of skilled personnel, assigned the human resources available primarily to those tasks regarded as priorities for the country's future, such as building up and operating a central administration. As a result the administrative structure of social security funds was very often set up in haste, with negative effects that have tended to perpetuate themselves ... While the higher ranks have increasingly been able to benefit ... from advanced specialised training within the framework of bilateral or multilateral co-operation, it is still extremely rare for the middle ranks and even more so for clerical and manipulative staff, without whom the funds cannot hope to operate properly, to have adequate training.[131]

---

129. Op. cit., Boulding, 1958.

130. Of course, this is a problem that plagues *all* organizations (public and private) during the initial stages of development.

High administrative costs

There has been concern raised in international circles with regard to the relatively high administrative costs of social security organizations in various countries. While it is difficult to compare large and small countries with a wide range of different programmes, those experts who have looked at the available data conclude that serious administrative inefficiencies in some countries are driving up costs and absorbing an excessive amount of incoming revenues. Mesa-Lago argues, for example:

> The percentage of administrative expenditure over total expenditure in the system is very high [for Latin America], fluctuating from 7 per cent in Costa Rica, Chile, and Uruguay to 10 per cent in Peru and 18 per cent in Mexico, percentages far above those in the developed countries. The majority of administrative expenditures relate to the remuneration of personnel, which is excessive in practically all of the countries.[132]

Contribution avoidance

Another major issue of administration is noncompliance by contributors (both governments and private employers) in the payment of contributions and the need for an adequate enforcement structure to deal with this situation.Experience shows that substantial policing is often required to ensure compliance among employers.Even where there is compliance, the payments may be deliberately delayed, especially in situations where interest rates and/or inflation are high.[133] In some countries, noncompliance is generally ignored; in others the penalties are not significant enough to encourage speedy compliance.

Low returns on reserves

While some countries operate their public pension programmes essentially on a pay-as-you-go basis, there are other countries where the social insurance programmes (or provident funds) accumulate sizeable reserves.In this regard, concerns have been raised about low rates of return on the investment portfolios. Reporting on eight Latin American countries, for example, Mesa-Lago

---

131. Jean-Victor Gruat. "Social Security Schemes in Africa: Current Trends and Problems," *International Labour Review*, vol. 129, no. 4 (1990): pp. 405-421, (p. 418).

132. Op. cit., Mesa-Lago, 1989, p. 254.

133. The ILO reports, for example, that there have been "record high levels of non-payment [in the Americas]: in Barbados, 44 per cent of payments are late; in Brazil, delays and evasion are of the order of 60 per cent; in Jamaica, delays are at 44 per cent; in Peru, evasion is at 33 per cent."See International Labour Office. *Social Security and the Process of Economic Restructuring*. Report II, 13th Conference of American States, Members of the ILO.

finds that only three of the eight countries had a positive average annual real yield on investments from public pension reserves.[134]

> This poor performance is partly due to rapid inflation, but it is also partly due to the governments' insistence that social security funds be invested in government papers. Such policies not only hide fiscal deficits, but also falsely reduce the cost of government borrowing. They have also resulted in decapitalization of pension funds. The purpose of pension funds is to finance future benefits, and the best way to do that is to secure the best possible rate of return to the investment portfolios.[135]

Dishonesty

Finally there is the issue of fraud and corruption. As with any programme that results in large transfers of money, there is a strong temptation for certain individuals to try to benefit illegally at the expense of the group. In many developing countries programmes have virtually collapsed as a result of funds being illegally diverted by administrators or government authorities for personal or other governmental uses. Administrators, employers, and workers are all potential violators. And programmes in developing countries are especially vulnerable — given that information gathering and record-keeping are more difficult and that legal processes for dealing with the problem are often underdeveloped and of low priority.

Competition and privatization

Is "competition" the answer to these administrative issues? With the recent decline in central planning in many countries and a consequent growing interest in market mechanisms, there has been increased interest in the possibilities of promoting competition in the provision of pensions. "Competition is the best possible means to ensure efficient resource allocation and performance," Kye Woo Lee of the World Bank told an ISSA conference in 1991.[136] "With competition, social security agencies would perform with more financial discipline and prudence, and the public and private sectors would develop their respective comparative advantage." The most common proposal for introducing competition is through "privatization" of government-run activities. By

---

134. Carmelo Mesa-Lago, *Portfolio Performance of Selected Social Security Institutes in Latin America*, World Bank Discussion Papers, 139 (Washington, DC: International Bank for Reconstruction and Development/World Bank, 1991).

135. Op. cit., Kye Woo Lee, 1991, p. 6.

136. Ibid.

shifting from public to private management, the aim is to boost organizational efficiency and raise the quality of the products/services provided.[137]

It is certainly true that competitive markets have shown themselves to be powerful incentive mechanisms to make people work hard, and to respond to the market demands (preferences) of buyers — thereby promoting efficiency. But privatization does not guarantee competition, and competition, if in fact it exists, does not guarantee honesty.

Given that effective competition is significantly weakened in many sectors by the growth and dominance of large firms, it is not surprising that privatization in many countries has been, in fact, the turning of public monopolies into private monopolies. Moreover, as Vickers and Yarrow show, there are flaws endemic in *both* private and public ownership.[138] With regard to private ownership, managers are often driven to strategies and practices that make essential products/services (e.g., health, education, drugs, etc.) unaffordable or unavailable to large segments of the population. Moreover, as the recent wave in some industrialized countries of "leveraged buyouts" (LBOs) indicates, privatization alone is not sufficient to guarantee appropriate business activity in the public interest.[139] "Takeover artists like Carl Icahn saw the same excesses in corporations that many people see in governmental entities: high wages, excess staffing, poor quality, and an agenda at odds with the goals of shareholders."[140]

As Goodman and Loveman point out, in addition to value for money paid, individuals want *access*, adherence to *performance standards*, and a *lack of corruption*.[141] This is certainly true in the case of public and private pensions for old age.

In this regard, the experience of industrialized countries that rely in a major way on employer-sponsored pensions is illuminating. These countries have had to create elaborate public regulatory structures and pension guarantee mechanisms to ensure promised benefits will be paid — given the history of misrep-

---

137. See, for example, Raymond Vernon. *The Promise of Privatization* (NY: Council on Foreign Relations, 1988). Vernon provides extensive information on some recent privatization activities in developing countries.

138. John Vickers and George Yarrow, "Economic Perspectives on Privatization," *Journal of Economic Perspectives,* vol. 5 (2), (Spring 1991): pp. 111-132.

139. Michael Jensen, "Eclipse of the Public Corporations," *Harvard Business Review,* vol. 89 (September-October, 1989): pp. 61-74.

140. John B. Goodman and Gary W. Loveman, "Does Privatization Serve the Public Interest?" *Harvard Business Review,* vol. 91 (November-December 1991): pp. 26-38, (p. 35).

141. Ibid, p. 36.

resentation, fraud, abuse, mismanagement, and so forth that caused major public dissatisfaction.[142] Of course, the vast majority of plans have been free of major problems, but there has always been a significant minority of plan administrators whose activities have necessitated the public supervision and the creation of large regulatory agencies.

For example, in the now often cited case of Chile's compulsory savings programme (that replaced its old social insurance programme), we find substantial government involvement. There is Chilean government approval of investor organizations, legislation severely restricting investment practices, major supervisory oversight (on a daily basis!) of the private investment firms' investment activities, and a number of government guarantees to protect the workers' personal pension accounts from mismanagement. These government practices are particularly important as doubts arise with regard to whether there is meaningful competition among investment firms. The proportion of Chilean workers with their savings in the top three firms rose from 60 per cent in 1981 to 67 per cent in 1991, while at the same time commissions were high and investment returns tended to be lower than in the smaller investment companies.[143]

Privatization and competition in practice does not guarantee that there will be no dishonesty in various industries. Moreover, the specific empirical evidence for *both* private and public pensions clearly indicates that neither is immune from this problem.

To illustrate the point that problems arise in all countries, we need only point to a recent example of the type of problem that can arise in an industrialized country. Before his death, super-financier Robert Maxwell, in a desperate attempt to prop up his debt-ridden communications empire, apparently illegally removed at least £400 million from various employee pension funds — making it almost certain that many workers covered by these plans will not get all the pension income to which they are entitled.[144]" Other directors and managers of the funds helped, turned a blind eye or were powerless to stop him."[145] The Maxwell example is just one recent, headline producing, example of the many

---

142. Op. cit., Schulz, 1992; op. cit., Hannah, 1986; Merton Bernstein. *The Future of Private Pensions* (New York: Free Press, 1964).

143. See, for example, the discussion in op. cit., Mesa-Lago, 1989.

144. "An Honour System without Honour", *Economist* (December 14, 1991): pp. 81-82; "The Maxwell Mess — Worsening", *Economist* (February 1, 1992): p. 91.

145. Op. cit., *Economist*, December 14, 1991, p. 82.

problems that arise in the management of public and private pension funds around the world.[146]

Unfortunately, the regulation that attempts to deal with the problems does not come cheaply and is only as good as its regulators — as anyone knows who is familiar with facts surrounding the US$200-500 billion in taxpayer funds currently being paid out to rescue depositors in the "savings and loan" and general banking institutions of the United States. As Kuttner correctly points out, "you can't contract out a service efficiently without having a force of competent civil servants to monitor the contractor. If you cut government to the bone, the contractor ends up with all the knowledge — and the theoretical option of replacing him with a competing vendor evaporates."[147]

Economic issues

The economic literature with regard to the impact of pensions is dominated by two issues: (a) the effect of pensions on saving and capital formation and (b) their effect on the supply of labour. Aaron and Thompson have argued that the major economic effects of social insurance depend to a large extent on two major behavioural alternatives: "'Life cycle' households plan the allocation of all resources available to them on the basis of their own wants, which may or may not include utility derived from bequests or gifts. 'Multigenerational' households allocate the resources available to them *and their heirs* to maximize their own *and their heirs'* wellbeing."[148] If individuals have multigenerational planning horizons, Aaron and Thompson show that theoretical models predict that social insurance will have little effect on savings and labour supply behaviour. In contrast, if a life cycle perspective dominates, theoretical models predict that social insurance will produce lower saving or lower labour supply (or both).

After considerable empirical research and debate over the results in industrialized countries, economists have *not* been able to agree on the actual effects of various pension schemes on savings and capital formation. In contrast, there is now a fairly high amount of agreement on the question of what happens to the labour supply when various types of pensions are introduced.

---

146. For the United States, see "SSA: Just Another Bureaucracy You Can't Trust?" in Chapter 5 of op. cit., Schulz, 1992; Frank Lalb. "The Empty Promise of Annuities," *Money* (April 1992): p. 7.

147. Robert Kuttner, "Privatization is Not a Cure-All," *Wall Street Journal* (April 30, 1992): A13.

148. Op. cit., Aaron and Thompson, 1987, p. 88.

Savings

With regard to the savings issue, a flurry of research activity on pensions and savings began in 1974 with a controversial study by American economist Martin Feldstein.[149] Feldstein's econometric study concluded that growing social insurance coverage and benefit levels in the United States may have reduced total personal savings. Lesnoy and Leimer then called attention to a serious error in Feldstein's study and reached the opposite conclusion (i.e., no impact from social insurance on net personal savings) using the same data.[150] Barro argued that historically social security has changed the pattern of voluntary intergenerational transfers (from parents to children and vice versa) and presented statistical evidence in support of the "no impact" findings that indicated changing patterns of family transfers were offsetting the reduced savings impact of social security.[151] Numerous other studies followed these initial studies.[152] The results have been inconclusive, with almost no evidence to date indicating that social security significantly reduces personal saving.[153] As Nicholas Barr points out, individuals' *expectations* play a key role in the savings impact outcome, and "since the formation of expectations is unmeasurable, the issue remains unresolved."[154]

Over the years there has been interest in some developing countries with regard to using pensions as one mechanism for accumulating savings for capital

149. Martin Feldstein. "Social Security, Induced Retirement, and Aggregate Capital Accumulation," *Journal of Political Economy*, vol. 83 (June 1975): pp. 447-475.

150. Selig D. Lesnoy and D. R. Leimer. "Social Security and Private Saving: New Time Series Evidence with Alternative Specifications," Working Paper No. 22 (Washington, DC: Office of Research and Statistics, US Social Security Administration, 1979).

151. Robert J. Barrow. *The Impact of Social Security on Private Savings — Evidence from the U.S. Time Series* (Washington, DC: American Enterprise Institute, 1978).

152. One of the most recent is Alan Auerbach, Robert Nicolette, and Laurence J. Kotlikoff. "The Economics of Aging Populations: The Case of Four OECD Economies," *OECD Economic Studies* (Spring 1989).

153. See the summary in Henry J. Aaron. *Economic Effects of Social Security* (Washington, DC: The Brookings Institution, 1982; for a summary of research in 16 OECD countries see Erkki Koskela and Matti Viren. "Social Security and Household Saving in an International Cross Section," *American Economic Review*, vol. 73 (March 1983): pp. 212-217; for a review of employer-sponsored plans and savings in the U.S., see Alicia H. Munnell and F.O. Yohn. "What Is the Impact of Pensions in Savings?" in Zvi Bodie and Alicia H. Munnell. *Pensions and the Economy: Sources, Uses, and Limitations of Data* (Philadelphia, PA:Pension Research Council of University of Pennsylvania Press, 1992), pp. 115-148.

154. Nicholas Barr. "Economic Theory and the Welfare State: A Survey and Interpretation," *Journal of Economic Literature*, vol. 30 (June 1992): pp. 741-803.

formation. But the record of countries actually investing social security reserves has not been good.

Labour supply disincentives

The research experience regarding pensions and labour supply has been radically different. While some amount of controversy again exists, there is a much larger measure of consensus among economists that pensions *reduce the supply of labour*.[155] We now have considerable historical perspective on this phenomenon in industrialized countries. Economists are inclined to view with concern policies that discourage work and thereby possibly impact negatively on a nation's output capacity and economic growth. But in fact, there is now a long history of using pensions as a labour supply "buffer" to deal with cyclical and structural adjustment problems in market-oriented countries.[156] When problems in these areas have arisen, retirement policies related to social insurance and employer-sponsored pensions have played a dominant role in helping to balance the demand and supply of labour. As expressed by Dan Jacobson, "more and more governments and unions have ... come to recognize that adopting employment buffering strategies or developing worker-oriented adjustments and job-replacement strategies are a vital and, indeed, expedient element in human resource policies."[157]

We would expect that pensions would play similar roles in developing countries in the years to come. That is, it is likely that developing countries will not be so concerned about retaining the aged in the labour force but rather will be seeking ways to adjust the supply and demand for labour in more humane ways than currently. A major concern for both industrialized and developing countries, in this regard, is the phenomenon of "early retirement."

---

155. A good summary of much of the economic literature is found in Joseph F. Quinn, Richard V. Burkhauser, and D. C. Myers. *Passing the Torch: The Influence of Economic Incentives on Work and Retirement* (Kalamazoo, MI: Upjohn Institute for Employment Research, 1990). See also, the earlier review by A. B. Atkinson. "Income Maintenance and Social Insurance," in Alan Auerbach and Martin Feldstein, eds. *Handbook of Public Economics*, vol. 2 (Amsterdam: North-Holland, 1987).

156. Op. cit., Schulz, 1991 (in Myles and Quadagno, 1991).

157. Dan Jacobson. "Optional Early Retirement: Is It a Painless Alternative to Involuntary Layoffs?" in S. Bergman, G. Naegele, and W. Tokarski, eds. *Early Retirement; Approaches and Variations: An International Interpretation* (Israel and Germany: Joint Publication of the Brookdale Institute of Gerontology and Human Development and Soziale Gerontologie Fachbereich Sozialwesen Gesamthochschule Universität Kassel, 1988).

Labour force participation rates for older *men* have been declining around the world, especially in industrialized countries.[158] Moreover, since the early 1970s many OECD countries have witnessed dramatic declines in labour force participation rates for men 50 to 64 years old.[159] The cost of this "early retirement" is measured not only by the costs of pensions paid out, but also by the reduced economic output resulting when fewer workers remain in the work force. The use of pensions as a major device for *labour supply buffering* (discussed above) conflicts with the more fundamental need to keep people working to maintain economic output at levels sufficient to meet a nation's goals for adequate, equitable, and rising incomes (i.e., rising living standards). The desire of most people to retire as early as possible — together with labour, employer, and government policies to encourage older workers to leave at very early ages — threatens to result in a too rapid growth in the older non-working population and a concurrent major shift in total output to meet their "retirement needs."Concern is growing, in part because of growing early retirement promises, about the "burden" of the aged and potential intergenerational conflict over the division of the national output.[160]

Trust: The foundation of social insurance

The provision of economic security through social insurance relies very heavily on trust. When people talk about social insurance "solidarity," "actuarial soundness," the "intergenerational compact," benefit equity, administrative efficiency, informational "transparency," solvency and integrity risks, and so forth — they are in large part talking about the trust people place in the future promises of the social insurance approach. Social insurance is a way of dealing with a variety of risks all individuals face (albeit some more than others). Its ability to deal with these risks depends on a variety of factors, many of which we have discussed above. But basic to the success of social insurance is the trust that people place in the institution itself. Without it, its viability is at great risk.

This need for trust is certainly not unique to social insurance. It is a need common to most financial institutions. For example, the fundamental basis of the acceptance of paper money in any society is the trust or belief of individuals

---

158. Trends for older women are mixed; one generally finds increases in their participation at ages 60-64 and small declines after age 64 B.B. Torrey, K. Kinsella, and C.M. Taeuber. *An Aging World*. International Population Reports, Series P-95, No. 78 (Washington, DC: U.S. Government Printing Office, 1987), Table 9.

159. Op. cit. Kohli, et al., 1991.

160. Op. cit., Pifer and Bronte, 1986; Schulz, Borowski, and Crown, 1991.

that other individuals will accept the money — not, as some believe, any precious metal "backing" for the money, the government's "stamp of approval," or some official edict of the central bank.

Lack of trust in a social insurance system undermines its viability in a variety of ways. For example, individuals who do not believe they will get promised benefits, or are not covered by the programme, are unlikely to support it politically. If governments continue to fall behind in the payments they are required under law to pay on behalf of their employees, they set an extremely poor example for other employers. Administrative corruption and graft not only reduces political support but is likely to increase payroll tax avoidance and recipient fraud. And the lack of explicit actions to protect social insurance pensions from the ravages of inflation seriously undermines support and compliance.

In all these examples and the many others that could be cited, the lack of trust promotes self-interested behavior that encourages individuals and groups to push for special consideration and benefits at the expense of others. The result is often political activities that seek to shift the problems of economic security to another arena.[161] The result is a fractionalized system of protection that often results in wide variation in the adequacy of programmes for various groups in the country.

There are positive steps that countries can take to promote trust. One key action that can be taken is a public review of financial and administrative operations. The experience in the industrialized countries indicates that *it is vitally important that any social insurance programme have an effective set of mechanisms for reviewing the general operations of the programme and especially for assessing the financial integrity of the fiscal operations.* This is done — in different ways in different countries — through a variety of committees, boards, advisory groups, and actuarial reviews.

Each developing country needs to pay serious attention to the mechanisms for review that currently exist and consider ways of improving them. All too often, the financial conditions of the social insurance programme have been

---

161. Peter Thullen makes this observation for Latin America. See his article: "El Financiamiento de Regimenes Obligatorios de Pensiones bajo Condiciones Dinamicas y las Nuevas Matematicas Actuariales," *Seguridad Social,* vol. 31 (May-August 1982); Tamburi discusses the same phenomenon with regard to Eastern Europe. See his article, op. cit., 1992.

allowed to deteriorate to the point that remedial action is not only difficult but sometimes impossible without major changes to the system of economic support.[162]

* * * * * * * * * * * *

The need for social protection is growing, not diminishing, around the world — in both developed and developing countries. In fact, the rising tide of market solutions to economic development issues promises an accelerating need for mechanisms that assist individuals in dealing with the risks and social disruptions arising out of social, demographic, political, and economic change.

We have tried to show in this publication that there is no one ideal mechanism that responds to these needs without generating a set of its own problems. We also showed that there are many important reasons why the social insurance mechanism has been the major mechanism of choice in so many countries throughout the world.

Hence, we must avoid an "either-or" approach to policymaking in this area. Given the problems confronting social insurance programmes around the world, some would have us "give up" on this approach and switch to some other alternative. However, since all options have major problems, it seems appropriate to continue with a multi-pillar approach, emphasizing the complementarity of mechanisms and dealing explicitly with the often difficult integration issues that result.

A big job remains in almost every country to improve social insurance. Moreover, since no one approach is perfect, each country (given its unique culture, history, development level, etc.) needs to determine what is the appropriate *mix* of social insurance with the various other options enumerated at the beginning of this document.

---

162. This is the explanation for the abolition of the Chilean social insurance programme in the early 1980s. See, for example, the discussion in Robert J. Myers. "Privatization of Chile's Social Security Program," *Benefits Quarterly,* vol. 1, No. 3 (1985): pp. 26-35.

Acknowledgements

My sincere appreciation goes to those who read earlier drafts of this monograph and provided me with reaction, corrections, and encouragement:

Ehtishan Ahmad, International Monetary Fund

Roger A. Beattie, International Labour Organization

Dalmer Hoskins, International Social Security Association

John McCallum, Australian National University

William McGreevey, World Bank

Carmelo Mesa-Lago, University of Pittsburgh

Robert J. Myers, Social Security Consultant

Stanford G. Ross, Arnold and Porter

Winfried Schmähl, University of Bremen

Donald Shepard, Brandeis University

Giovani Tamburi, Watson Europe

Martin B. Tracy, University of Iowa

John Williamson, Boston College

Dimitri Vittas, World Bank

3

Structural adjustment and social security: The interaction[1]

Colin Gillion
Director, Social Security Department
International Labour Office

During the 1980s a large number of countries throughout the world adopted programmes of structural adjustment and reform. Of course, structural change and adaptation to it are continuous processes, occupying the attention of policy makers in all countries at all times. But what was unique about the 1980s was the extent to which governments deliberately initiated policies aimed at basic, and sometimes radical, changes in the framework of their economies: their structure, management, the approach to economic policy, and above all, in the fundamental rules of the game. Almost invariably, and in contrast to previous decades, changes in the latter have involved a reduced role for direct public intervention and regulation, a move towards economies which are more open to world trade and development, and a greater reliance on market forces and competitive pressures.

---

1. The following paper draws heavily on material prepared by Roger Beattie and Michael Cichon of the Social Security Department of the International Labour Office, but neither they nor the International Labour Office are necessarily committed to the views expressed, which are the author's personal responsibility.

Such changes have implications for the role of social protection policies. On the one hand, the new economic structures and the process of transition towards them have placed different and additional demands on social programmes. On the other hand, the presence of adequate systems of social protection has had considerable influence on the acceptability of structural reforms and has helped to shape the social consensus which has widened the purely economic process into one involving greater political democracy and attention to human rights. The changes have also raised questions about the efficiency and effectiveness of the social programmes themselves, their management and financial viability, and about their broader context, in particular their relationship to labour market and training programmes.

The purpose of this short paper is to sketch briefly some of the background to these reforms, their social consequences and their interaction with programmes of social security and social protection, and to raise some of the main issues for policy discussion.

The economic background

Behind the rapid increase in the number of countries undertaking economic reforms or structural adjustment policies during the 1980s lies a considerable divergence in experience between the various regions and countries of the world economy. On the one hand, the developed countries have grown much more rapidly than the developing countries (with the exception of some Asian countries). On the other hand, prolonged stagnation among the centrally planned economies of Central and Eastern Europe led, in the closing years of the decade, to the adoption of comprehensive reforms — political and social as well as economic — aimed at their structural transition to a market-oriented economy.

These divergencies have had a fundamental bearing on both the timing and extent of structural adjustment policies in the various countries and regions, and require some further amplification.

In sharp contrast to the sustained growth and high employment of the 1960s and early 1970s, the **developed** free-market economies (i.e., the OECD countries) experienced a period of slow growth from the mid-1970s into the early 1980s. The prima facie cause for this slow-down was the sharp rise in oil prices. Policy reactions in the first instance were largely reflationary, as governments attempted to compensate for the income losses inherent in the altered terms of trade. After 1975 the initial policy stance was fairly quickly reversed and replaced by policies which emphasised fiscal constraint and tight monetary conditions, and whose overriding objective was the restoration of non-inflationary growth. Progress in adjusting economies and policies was slow, but 1982-1983 marked a turning point. It is expected that between 1982 and 1992, real GDP for the OECD countries will have increased by just over 35 per cent. For the same period, inflation rates will probably average just over 4 per cent per annum. But unemployment rates are likely to remain high, at just over 7 per cent of the labour force in 1991 and 1992.

Underlying these macro-economic developments were a number of significant structural changes, partly reflecting exogenous changes in demography, technology and relative prices, partly the result of conscious policy decisions. The labour market has become fragmented, many governments have pursued conscious policies of privatization, social expenditures have come under severe constraint (and in some areas, reform), and many governments have adopted programmes of tax reform which emphasize greater simplicity and lower marginal rates.

Finally, it should be noted that the domestic climate within the developed economies has not been propitious for an expansion of development aid.

In contrast to the growth which occurred in the developed countries during the 1980s, per capita GDP among the **developing** countries of Sub-Saharan Africa and in Latin America declined during the 1980s. Among the developing countries of Europe, the Middle East and North Africa, per capita growth was very low. Only East and South Asian countries as a region experienced growth rates comparable to those in the developed countries, and even here the experience was very mixed.

To a large extent, the declines in the developing countries resulted from factors outside their immediate control. During the 1980s their terms of trade declined severely — by over 5 per cent per annum for Sub-Saharan Africa, by just over 4 per cent per annum in Latin America, and just under 4 per cent per annum in the developing countries of Europe, Middle East and North Africa. Particularly for Sub-Saharan Africa, increases in export volumes were insufficient to make up for this deterioration. Financing the external deficits became harder — dramatically so in the cases of some developing countries. The increase in external debt during the 1970s had been spectacular: 23 per cent per annum in the case of Sub-Saharan Africa, 21 per cent per annum in Latin America, and nearly 29 per cent per annum in Europe, North Africa and the Middle East. Corresponding growth rates during the period 1980 to 1986 were lower. But the higher real interest rates which prevailed from 1980 onwards applied not only to new debt but also to the debt outstanding at the beginning of the decade. Largely as a result of the need to service both the new and the old debt, net transfers to developing countries fell very sharply indeed: from an inflow of around $US 27 billion in 1980 to an outflow of around $US 26 billion by the end of the decade.

The impact of these two developments — the decline in the terms of trade and the difficulty of debt servicing, against a background of declining real output — formed a major external compulsion for the governments of developing countries to adopt strategies of structural adjustment during the 1980s. This they did in growing numbers: some few countries of their own volition, but most in association with — if not at the behest of — international agencies such as the IMF and the World Bank who provided the financial cover for the international commitments. But an equally important compulsion arose from the cumulative effect of policies and economic structures which had been inherited from the 1960s and 1970s and which were inappropriate to the altered circumstances of the 1980s. In addition to macro-economic policies which displayed an excessive reluctance to deal with short-term imbalances (in terms of inflation or balance of payments deficits), for many developing countries these included:

- overvalued exchange rates, coupled with excessively high tariffs and quantitative controls on imports;

- excessively low interest rates (frequently negative in real terms) coupled with credit rationing;

- permanently high fiscal deficits, associated with excessively high public sector employment;

- large scale public commitment to and support of unprofitable state-owned enterprises;

- widespread price controls; and

- consumer subsidies, particularly of basic commodities and foods.

These features took their most extreme form, of course, in the centrally planned economies of **Central and Eastern Europe** and were associated with a long period during which the supply side of these economies first stagnated and then eventually broke down. This has led, over the last two or three years, to the radical political, economic and social changes which are intended as precursors to their transition to market-oriented economies. The full structural transition is obviously some way away: for the moment, the main issues are those associated with the immediate stabilization of the economies, including the emergence of substantial inflation and unemployment and a sharp fall in output.

Stabilization and structural adjustment

Programmes of economic stabilization are generally aimed at the immediate elimination of imbalances within the economy, such as large and unsustainable deficits in the balance of payments and in the public accounts, or the eradication of rapid inflation of prices and wages. The main instruments employed tend to be those of macro-economic policy, in particular fiscal and monetary restraint. Structural adjustment programmes on the other hand are intended to be longer acting and are broadly aimed at the removal of economic distortions which have grown up over time as the result of government policy and intervention. Distortion in this sense is understood as the divergence between the actual structure of institutions and prices (as determined by government policies, regulations and institutions), and those which would prevail in a situation of un-modified market forces, competition and the absence of government intervention and regulation. Particular attention is usually paid to the alignment of domestic prices and structures with those of the world economy. The measures adopted under structural adjustment programmes include, among others, the freeing of exchange rate and interest rate mechanisms, the removal of price controls and subsidies, the reduction of tariffs and quantitative controls on imports and the removal of export subsidies, the privatization of parastatal enterprises, deregulation of markets, including the labour market, and the reallocation of public expenditures, usually within a greatly reduced overall total. Although the immediate purpose of such reforms is both to establish a viable economic equilibrium and to ensure a more efficient allocation of resources, their main strategic aims are longer term: to put in place the necessary, if not sufficient, conditions for faster economic growth, higher levels of employment, and better standards of living.

At least in the short term however, programmes of economic stabilization and structural adjustment have had adverse social consequences, particularly on the poor and the lower paid members of society. These have been identified in a number of ILO meetings (the High-Level Meeting on Employment and Structural Adjustment, Geneva, November 1991; the Tripartite Symposium on Structural Adjustment and Employment in Africa, Nairobi, October 1989; the Tripartite Symposium on Structural Adjustment, Employment and Training in Latin America and the Caribbean, Caracas, August 1991; and the Eleventh Asian Regional Conference, Bangkok, November-December 1991). For workers in the formal sector, the principal adverse effects include higher unemployment and underemployment and falling real wages. For the population at large, programmes of structural adjustment have been associated with increasing poverty, and cuts in spending on health, education and food subsidies. Frequently such adverse effects are superimposed on an initially unfavourable economic situation, either in terms of a recent history of slow growth or in terms of permanent low incomes and a high incidence of poverty.

Whatever the mix, as between the consequences of structural adjustment policies, their context of slow economic growth, or the long-term existence of permanently low incomes, it is clear that during the 1980s and particularly for developing countries, the need for social protection has become greater at the same time that the resources for providing it have diminished. The funds available for developing tax-based programmes of social protection have been restricted as a result of government decisions on public expenditure. And falling wages and declining employment have reduced the revenue basis of contributory social security schemes. Moreover, shifts in relative prices, especially of basic commodities and necessities, have had a differential impact on various social groups, many of whom do not have the capacity to adjust to the new economic regime. Where such groups are already poor, the impact can be severe, and inequitably so. In only a few countries has the emergence of more rapid and equitably disbursed economic growth offset some of these adverse developments.

The institutions of social security

This situation has been exacerbated by a long-standing need for reform among the institutions and mechanisms of social protection themselves. Although many countries have a substantial history of social security institutions, their development has been neglected over previous decades and they lack the capacity to respond to the current situation. Coverage of the population is inadequate, the number of contingencies covered is in many cases limited, benefit levels are frequently very low (even relative to average incomes) and access to and the quality of services has deteriorated, especially in health care programmes. Above all, in many cases the administrative functioning of the schemes has declined to the point where they are incapable of delivering even the restricted potential which current economic circumstances allow. High administrative charges, evasion and the lack of compliance on the part of contributors, ineffectual and late payment of benefits, absence of adequate record keeping, lack of regional coverage, and in some cases straight corruption have added to the problems caused by the limited coverage and inappropriate design of the different social security systems.

Attempts in developing countries to restrain the growth of money supply and credit have created problems for many semi-autonomous social security institutions. In part the problems arose prior to programmes of structural adjustment, because high rates of inflation and low real interest rates have eroded the financial base of the institutions. Even where financial sector reforms have resolved some of these problems, they have still left many institutions without resources to meet additional demands (in the form mainly of pensions) and with a much reduced income base. The financial problems have in many cases been exacerbated by problems of management and compliance and the difficulty of recuperating contributions from employers and employees during a period of low incomes and unemployment.

The ILO's concept of "social security" has essentially been based on Convention No. 102 (1952) concerning minimum standards of social security. A working definition is as follows:

> The protection which society provides its members, through a series of public measures, against the economic and social distress that otherwise would be caused by the stoppage or substantial reduction of earnings resulting from sickness, maternity, employment injury, unemployment, invalidity, old-age and death; the provision of medical care; and the provision of subsidies for families with children.

The above definition principally refers to statutory schemes set up by law, which take one of the following forms:

- Social insurance schemes, which are financed mainly by insured persons' and employers' contributions and under which both the entitlement and the rate of benefit depend on the individual contribution record.

- Universal schemes, which are general revenue financed, and which provide benefits at standard rates to all residents of specified categories.

- National provident funds, which are in the nature of compulsory savings schemes; members' and their employers' contributions are accumulated in individual accounts, with interest, and paid out, typically in lump-sum form, on the occurrence of one of the specified contingencies.

- Employer-liability schemes, under which specified categories of employers are obliged by law to provide specified benefits to their employees.

- Social assistance schemes, which provide means-tested benefits out of general revenue, and generally act as a second line of defence to afford a measure of protection to those who fall outside the scope of the main scheme or receive inadequate benefits from the main scheme.

The emphasis in the above working definition is on statutory schemes, set up by law. However non-statutory schemes, in particular occupational pension schemes or health schemes, are of considerable importance in certain countries. The concept of "social protection schemes" adopted by the EEC, is wider than the ILO concept of "social security". In particular, it includes non-statutory schemes and covers contingencies not included in Convention 102 (e.g. benefits in respect of resettlement, placement, vocational guidance and housing).

In fact, provision of income security in old age is provided mainly through social insurance schemes or provident funds, of which the latter are mostly found in the formerly UK administered countries. The lump-sum provident fund benefit bears no relation to the social need of the beneficiary, and this type of scheme does not involve any risk-pooling. Accordingly, several provident funds have been considering their transformation into pension schemes. But little progress has been made due to a range of psychological, administrative and technical reasons. Both social insurance pension schemes and provident funds, which accumulate very substantial reserve funds, need to invest their funds in secure outlets providing at least a non-negative real rate of return. Unfortunately, even these minimum conditions do not obtain in several developing countries. The schemes are often obliged to place their funds in government bonds yielding returns considerably below market rates. There are also cases where the funds are borrowed by the government without any conditions as to periodic returns or repayment of the capital. In these circumstances, the implied funding level at the origin of the scheme deteriorates over time, and the scheme tends to degenerate into an unfunded pay-as-you-go scheme. This means that the brunt of increasing benefit costs due to the maturation of the scheme must be borne by current contributions which consequently are higher than originally anticipated.

The structural adjustment process has placed additional strains on some of the already ailing pension schemes. The increased unemployment resulting from the adjustment process has meant a reduction in the contributing population. On the other hand, temporary measures to alleviate the situation of redundant workers, for example through early retirement provisions, has produced a rapid increase in the number of beneficiaries. In some countries, the national social security scheme has been obliged to incorporate persons retrenched from the contracting civil service under specially adopted voluntary insurance provisions, which will enable the beneficiaries to earn pensions after relatively short periods of affiliation.

An additional aspect concerns inefficiencies in the collection of contributions. In many countries the institution is required to pay to the insured persons all benefits which have been earned in virtue of contributions, including those contributions which have not been received due, for example, to the delinquency of the employer. This places on the scheme a strain which was not anticipated at the planning stage. This aspect becomes more acute during periods of recession and also during the period of structural adjustment. In some cases, export-oriented industries are encouraged by a special dispensation permitting a partial remission of statutory social security contributions for specified time periods, without reducing the benefit accruals in virtue of the corresponding contribution periods, a feature which clearly adds to the difficulties encountered.

The social consequences

The general economic developments described above, the structural adjustment programmes put in place during the 1980s, and the management and operational difficulties encountered by the social security institutions, have together had important consequences for social conditions and for the need for policies of social protection.

The social impact of structural adjustment depends to a very great extent on the existing structure both of the economy and systems of social protection. In **developed** countries, elaborate systems of social protection were in place and universally applicable before the recession and the concurrent structural changes. To a very large degree, the social protection measures which were established during the 1960s and early 1970s enabled them to withstand the large scale rise in unemployment without losing either the consensus or the momentum for change. But for **developing** countries the situation was and is quite different. Two key features here appear to be the size of the formal sector, which largely determines the extent and coverage of self-supporting social security systems, and the revenue resources which governments can use to support generalized anti-poverty or health care programmes. For most developing countries, both vehicles of social protection are inadequate to provide effective coverage or levels of benefits, and have not enabled them to respond to the additional needs generated by structural adjustment programmes which have been superimposed on already difficult economic conditions. In Sub-Saharan Africa, for example, the formal sector covers less than 10 per cent of the active labour force: the proportion covered by social security schemes is very much less. Finally, for **Central and Eastern European** countries in transition to market-oriented systems, the social protection implicit in the former system of universal and obligatory employment, and channeled through state enterprises and unions, has now disappeared. Alongside the development of free and competitive labour markets, many aspects of the system of social protection need to be constructed almost from scratch, especially those needed to deal with a rapid growth in unemployment.

Some of the main types of impact and the social groups most vulnerable to them are as follows:

Labour market repercussions

The most serious and most pervasive effects of both stabilization and structural adjustment programmes are felt in the labour market. For the developed countries this has chiefly meant rising unemployment, but also slower growth in real wages and a weakening of the position of marginal or disadvantaged social groups. For the developing countries, the situation has been different. The recession brought with it a considerable deceleration in the growth of urban, formal sector employment, particularly in Sub-Saharan Africa, and with it increased difficulties in providing income maintenance even for those experiencing open unemployment. At the same time, the size of the urban labour force continued to grow very rapidly.

Public sector employment

Policies of reducing government expenditure, coupled with extensive privatization of state owned enterprises, has resulted in large scale redundancies in public sector employment (for example Sri Lanka, Trinidad, Benin). In both developed and developing countries, public servants tend to be among the most highly protected sector of the labour force, frequently enjoying both redundancy and pension rights considerably better than those in the private sector. Retrenchment of public sector employment have not only raised questions about redundancy and unemployment benefits, but has also placed severe demands on pension schemes in response to early retirement programmes.

Social expenditures

Public expenditure constraints have resulted in significant declines in public social expenditures, particularly those on publicly financed health care programmes and education. In Sub-Saharan Africa, per capita social expenditures declined in real terms by almost 40 per cent between 1978 and 1985. And in a sample of Latin American countries, only Chile has shown significant growth in social spending during the 1980s, with a number of other countries showing severe declines, not only in real capita terms but also as a proportion of total government expenditures.

Poverty

Structural adjustment programmes have frequently been associated with increases in the general level of poverty, although as with other aspects, it is difficult to distinguish between the effects of the programmes themselves and the general background of economic crisis. However, experience has differed very sharply as between different types of countries and, within countries, between different social groups. In **developed** countries, poverty rates among the retired and elderly have declined, mainly as a consequence of the very rapid growth in public expenditure on pensions which governments found it almost impossible to constrain as a result of past promises and accrued entitlements. But poverty rates among marginalized groups (in particular, among the growing number of single parent families) increased noticeably. A disturbing feature has been the increase in poverty among individuals who are still in employment but with very low wages. These changes have been associated with structural changes in the labour market, in family and household structure, and higher prevailing levels of unemployment, have meant a significant shift in the pattern of dependency within the community and hence, in the relative distribution of household incomes. They also mean that, cumulatively, there has developed a mismatch between the current realities and the assumptions — about employment and family structures — on which social security systems are currently based. And while the conventional concepts implied that the needs for income maintenance, employment and training could be treated as separate issues, the post 1980 realities demanded otherwise.

The net outcome of these changes has been to reduce the overall level of dependency: measured, that is, by numbers employed as a proportion of total population. In effect, increased female participation rates have outweighed the other trends. But more importantly, the burden of support for dependents has shifted substantially away from private, mainly intra-family, transfers and towards systems of public support. By comparison with a decade or so earlier, the households which have increased their independence and their private incomes are those intact families in the middle age-range: they now have fewer children and a higher proportion have two earners. Families with children in the age-range 16 to 25 are finding that the need for support has increased. In contrast, the increase in the number of households where the man has retired early, which are headed by a single mother, or which include one or more unemployed is placing greater demands on social security transfers and reducing the base of public revenues.

Poverty in **developing** countries has also increased, and for many of the same reasons which have influenced poverty in developed countries, in particular the weakness of the labour market, the decline in formal sector employment, and declines in real wages. In addition, the position of the poor in many developing countries has been adversely affected by the removal of price controls and subsidies on basic commodities, and because of shifts and changes in prices between rural and urban sectors as a result of changes in exchange rates and tariffs.

One important and widely-used method of protecting poor and vulnerable groups in society in many developing countries is by guaranteeing their food security — that is, by making sure that they can acquire adequate food at all times. There exists a wide range of food subsidy schemes: general food price subsidies, food rations, food stamps, food distribution policies and food supplementation schemes. However, the coverage, scope and even existence of such schemes has been questioned and reduced in many countries during periods of economic stabilization that place a premium on reducing government expenditure and thereby reining in the fiscal deficit. Moreover, in countries where the aim of structural adjustment policies is to alter the prices or incentive arrangements that exist, so as to encourage farmers to substitute the production of tradeable agricultural commodities for those that are consumed domestically and thereby reduce the balance of payments deficit, emphasis is often placed on limiting or removing food subsidies.

The reduction or removal of food subsidies, along with devaluation and public sector retrenchments, is one of the most controversial aspects of structural adjustment programmes in the countries concerned, and in several cases has been the spark that has led to popular protest and riots against the government and its economic policies. The reasons for this are clear. Subsidies are highly visible, and their alteration can lead to significant and instant changes in living standards. This is because price reductions caused by subsidy programmes are often large. It is not uncommon to find that the subsidy reduces the consumer prices by half or more, as exemplified by subsidies for wheat, sugar and beans in Egypt and edible oil in the Philippines. It is obvious that the actual effect of food subsidies on the real incomes of the poor will depend on the nature of the subsidy schemes, the choice of commodities to be subsidized, and the design and implementation of the distribution scheme. However, it has been estimated that in several programmes, the value of food subsidies received by low income households accounts for 15 to 25 per cent of their total real income.

By the same token, food subsidies can be extremely costly for the government. This is particularly the case with general food price subsidy schemes that supply unlimited amounts of subsidized food to anyone who wishes to buy it. Brazil, China, Colombia, Egypt, Mexico, Morocco, Pakistan, Sudan, Thailand and Tunisia are all examples of countries that have operated these types of schemes. In the case of Egypt, the World Bank has estimated that between the mid-1970s and mid-1980s between 10 and 17 per cent of total public expenditures in Egypt were devoted to general food subsidies.

As far as **Central and Eastern European** countries are concerned, all the former centrally planned economies provided a full range of social benefits and services, and for the most part these were universally available. They included retirement and invalidity pensions, health care services, family benefits, maternity grants and disability and sickness benefits. In addition, social aid programmes provided some assistance to the destitute. This range of traditional social benefits was extended to housing and, in some cases, towards the provision of holidays in specified resorts. The main omission was that of any developed system of unemployment compensation or universal minimum income provision. The feasibility of this kind of arrangement rested on the provisions of the employment laws. All citizens — both men and women — had both the right and the obligation to work. Those who did not work without some valid reason (such as invalidity) were very largely excluded from the social provisions. It was reasonably sure therefore, that an enterprise-based structure would encompass almost all the population and all those who possessed entitlements to benefits.

It appears almost self evident that these features of the former system of social protection are, or at least will be, incompatible with the new structure of the reformed economies; that they will not respond to the new needs which will emerge; and especially, that they will not contribute to the process of transition itself. A general reform — in fact reconstruction — of unemployment compensation and the safety nets is required. It is necessary to emphasize that there is no, or extremely little room, to respond to the social needs of the transition process by a net increase in public expenditures: all that can be hoped is that savings in other areas — industrial subsidies and so on — will provide scope for the establishment of at least some kind of safety net. But the immediate outlook is one in which the restructuring process will lead to rapidly increasing levels of unemployment. The picture is one in which a large number of job losses will occur, on account of a general economic stabilization programme, moves towards privatization and a market economy, and enterprises shedding part of their current "social employment" in response to tighter and more competitive budget constraints.

Problems and limits to the formal systems of protection

The vast majority of social security systems, in particular those based on social insurance, were not set up with the objective of providing benefits for poor people as such, far less of providing compensation for people adversely affected by structural adjustment programmes. This is not to say that they are of no relevance to the problems of poverty and development; it is simply to stress that they have various other objectives which cannot and should not be abandoned.

Their potential contribution to the success of structural adjustment is critically dependent on the proportion of the population that they cover. As we have seen, in most developing countries, that proportion is still very low and much thought has gone into possible ways of extending coverage. As far as income replacement benefits are concerned, the conclusion drawn by most experts is that it is generally extremely difficult to extend contributory social insurance schemes to cover the self-employed and people in the informal sector. Many of them could not afford to pay the contributions and, in any case, to ensure compliance would be a major administrative task. Furthermore, in most developing countries it is quite unrealistic to think that benefits for the entire population could be financed out of contributions paid by the small minority of the labour force working in the formal sector and currently covered by social security. More modest schemes may be possible among groups of the population that are to some extent organized or integrated into the modern sector. Social insurance coverage will increase, but only gradually as a larger proportion of the economically active population is drawn into the formal sector. It is, however worth mentioning that in recent years many countries have extended their social security schemes to cover all employers, having initially restricted coverage to larger establishments and/or to certain geographical areas. This has necessitated major efforts in terms of education and publicity, as well as a strengthening of inspectorates to ensure compliance.

Otherwise, social assistance benefits, or universal benefits where resources allow, are usually the only practical means to provide a measure of protection for those lying outside the scope of institutionalized social security. But in turn these rely on the existence of an effective and efficient source of tax revenue. In many developing countries, the collection of tax revenues faces similar problems to the collection of social insurance contributions: the tax base is small relative to the required expenditures; problems of enforcement and compliance may result in revenues greatly below their theoretical and legal potential; and questions of administrative costs, and in some countries, corruption, may erode the value of the revenues received.

The effectiveness of the benefits provided by social security schemes in developing countries has often left much to be desired. As a result, social protection even for the minority covered by such schemes has in many cases been inadequate. The shortcomings have taken a variety of forms. Some have been inherent in the legislation, while others have resulted from the legislation not being respected or from it being poorly implemented.

The effectiveness of social security schemes in cushioning the population from the effects of economic restructuring also depends on the regular index-ation of benefits. In this respect social security schemes in developing countries are generally deficient. Legislation often provides for some kind of benefit adjustment, but there is rarely any automatic mechanism to ensure that it actually takes place. However, under a reform implemented in January 1989, the Mexican social insurance system adjusts pensions in line with every increase in the general minimum wage, the principle of benefit indexation in line with earnings having been introduced a few years earlier in the scheme covering the country's public servants. The Social Security Law adopted in Ghana in 1991 states that the Social Security and National Insurance Trust "shall annually review the pension payment based on adjustment in salaries and wages of members"; this is more explicit than legislation in many other countries, but still stops short of giving any firm commitment.

To adjust benefits is thus a discretionary matter and those responsible for making the decision are often faced with financial problems if they do raise benefits in line with prices or wages. Part of the reason for this is that their schemes, unlike the pay-as-you-go social security systems in industrialized countries, often operate on a partially funded basis and the reserves which they have accumulated typically earn a very poor rate of return. In some cases, this may be attributed to lack of expertise in managing the funds, but more often it is a reflection of the fact that the schemes are not free to invest the funds as they judge best, but instead are obliged to invest in government paper often at negative real interest rates. Even if schemes are allowed to invest on the open market, they often find it very difficult to guarantee regular indexation of benefits, so long as they try to maintain the same degree of funding; funded pension schemes in the private sector of industrialised countries know this problem only too well. However, unlike private funded schemes, statutory schemes do at least have the possibility of solving the problem through the adoption of a pay-as-you-go system of financing. Another requirement, if benefits are to be indexed, is the regular indexation of any ceilings which may apply to contributions and benefits; there are countries in Africa, for instance, where ceilings have not been raised for decades, and where the real value of workers' pension entitlements has consequently declined steeply.

The non-indexation of benefit has also been a major problem in the countries of Central and Eastern Europe, where rapid inflation and swiftly changing relative prices have emerged as a consequence of price liberalization and the move towards more market oriented economies. The absence of any automatic mechanism to adjust benefits has left pensioners particularly vulnerable during periods of price deregulation. All countries in the region have, however, made ad hoc adjustments, generally with the aim of maintaining the real value of benefits at least at the bottom of the scale. Needless to say, the indexation of long-term benefits has major financial implications and social security systems in the countries of Central and Eastern Europe are having to consider to what extent they may have to reduce initial pension entitlements.

The effectiveness of social security administrations in ensuring compliance with legislation, particularly as regards the payment of contributions, has often fallen far short of 100 per cent, particularly in developing countries. This problem is making its appearance also in Central and Eastern Europe, as private sector activity starts to develop. The result is that social security coverage is rather less in practice than in theory. Certainly there is a shortfall in income from contributions, but this does not always seem to constitute a sufficient incentive for social security institutions to take action, perhaps because they know that the non-contributors will receive no benefits and that it is costly and time-consuming to chase them up if they work in very small establishments. The political will has to exist, if this problem is to be solved; a strong trade union movement can also help, although unions too are at usually at their weakest in small establishments.

There is certainly considerable scope for increasing the efficiency of social security administration in developing countries and international technical cooperation can make a major contribution in this respect. The aim should be not merely to reduce administrative costs as a percentage of revenue or expenditure, but also to improve the quality of service provided to insured persons. Accurate information about entitlements and prompt payment of benefits can transform the image of a social security scheme and may greatly increase people's willingness to pay contributions.

Reference has already been made to the need for governments of developing countries to increase the proportion of public expenditure devoted to social policies broadly defined (the UNDP's human expenditure ratio). Naturally government expenditure should be for the benefit of the population in general and for the most vulnerable in particular. For that reason, it is desirable that social insurance schemes, which in developing countries usually cover only a minority of the population, should be entirely self-financing. At the same time, there must be transparency in the dealings between the schemes and the governments; the latter must curb any tendency they may have had in the past to regard social security reserves as part of the general assets of the public sector.

Similarly, the distinction between social security (social insurance) contributions and taxes should be respected and maintained. Public acceptance of contributions depends on confidence that they are used for providing benefits to insured persons. If governments require additional revenue for other purposes, including social assistance, then transparency demands that this be collected in the form of taxation. The earnings-related benefits financed by social insurance contributions are sometimes criticized as a "privilege". However, it must be clearly realized that certain groups in any society feel the need for social protection and are willing to pay for it. Where statutory social insurance is not available, as for example in Zimbabwe, private occupational schemes have developed to provide, in particular, retirement pensions for employees in the formal sector. The difference is that private schemes do not cover all employees, leaving out lower paid and casual workers, the very people most likely to face poverty in retirement. Social insurance has the enormous advantage that it provides protection for all members of the target groups, regardless of their position on the income scale. Certain elements in social security systems, particularly in developed countries and in the countries of Central and Eastern Europe, may have undesirable effects on incentives and on the operation of the labour market. These should be reviewed, taking full account of economic and of social considerations, to ensure that social security supports rather than impedes the process of structural adjustment. But the matter is an empirical rather than a theoretical one. Care should obviously be taken to prevent workers receiving a higher net income when on benefit than in work (this may occur when benefits are tax free and earnings are subject to substantial tax and social security deductions). Early retirement provisions should be examined closely to ensure that they are not giving workers undue encouragement to quit their jobs early; and full consideration should be given to the economic and human costs of using early retirement as a measure to reduce short-term unemployment. But where benefits, especially those cash benefits which reflect basic safety nets and minimum incomes, are a significant distance away from the income which the recipient would earn from employment, then it may be assumed that the disincentive and inefficiency effects of the transfer payments are a less important consideration than the humanitarian objectives of preventing hardship and poverty.

Summary and conclusions

Programmes of economic stabilization and structural adjustment, together with weak economic growth and/or a deteriorating labour market, have added to the needs for social protection over recent years, particularly in developing countries and more recently in the countries of Central and Eastern Europe which are in the process of transition from planned to market-oriented economies. However the same features and circumstances have constrained, and in many cases reduced, the resources available to social programmes, both from general tax revenues and from social security contributions.

Among the social hardships imposed by programmes of stabilization and structural adjustment are:

- High levels of unemployment, concentrated among youth, older workers and the long-term unemployed in developed countries, and affecting the rate of growth of formal urban sector employment in developing countries.

- Poverty and low income among marginalized groups in the developed countries, increased rural poverty and among the urban poor in developing countries.

- Reduced spending on social programmes, particularly health care and education.

- Lower real wages, particularly for lower-paid workers, associated with a widening gap between the earnings of skilled and unskilled workers in developed countries.

- Reduced employment and increased redundancies among public sector employees as the result of reduced government expenditure and the privatization of state-owned enterprises.

- Lower standards of living among poorer sections of the community, especially in developing countries, as the result of lower subsidies on basic commodities and food, the removal of price controls, and exchange rate, tariff and quantity restrictions on imports.

In those countries where programmes of social security and social protection are well developed — mainly the advanced economies of the OECD area — social security systems have demonstrated their ability to cope effectively and efficiently with the consequences of recession and economic restructuring, and have alleviated many of the hardships which might otherwise have been experienced by the more disadvantaged social groups. Some gaps remain, chiefly those concerned with individuals excluded from the labour market or low income families with children. But the presence of an adequate social safety net has in fact contributed to the social consensus for economic change.

However, in many countries of Asia, Africa and Latin America, social security systems are not sufficiently developed to provide adequate support for the majority of the population affected by economic change or circumstances. Social security programmes in these countries provide some protection for workers in the formal sector: but even in the formal sector their coverage of all individuals or all contingencies is far from complete, and outside the formal sector it is frequently minimal.

Social protection programmes in such countries face a number of constraints. The weakness of the tax base and the need for fiscal restraint limits social expenditures from general public revenues. The small size of the formal sector limits the extent and coverage of conventional (contributory) social security schemes. Deficiencies in the administration, management and general governance of social security schemes frequently erode what can be achieved either by the collection of contributions or by the disbursement of benefits. And the existing political and social consensus for mechanisms of solidarity and income redistribution is often overstretched by the scale of the needs and by the size of the population at risk. Some of these constraints are binding, and are inherent to the state of development of the country concerned. But in many cases their severity could be softened, and the scope and level of benefits improved, by the establishment of appropriate policies or by the reform of the institutions of social protection.

Countries of Central and Eastern Europe face the problem that the level of social protection previously provided as part of the guarantee of full employment in state-owned enterprises must now be replaced by mechanisms and institutions which are adapted to those of the market economy. Paramount among the problems of transition is that of creating an adequate social safety net for those becoming unemployed. But the systems of old age pensions and those of health care services are in need of almost total revision, both to overcome a backlog of inadequacy and inefficiency and to respond to the new, market-oriented context, particularly the freeing of the labour market. That said, the countries of Central and Eastern Europe possess a tradition and structure of high levels of formal sector employment, a developed administrative structure, a context of social solidarity, and a potential for reform, all of which constitute a base from which can develop a strong and market-compatible welfare state.

The ultimate and long-term objectives in the area of social security and social protection should remain those embodied in the various International Labour Standards relating to the subject. Broadly, these envisage the establishment of adequate levels of benefits and social services for all members of the population and covering all contingencies. But for many countries the immediate situation and the general state of economic and social development mean that such objectives cannot be achieved in the near or medium-term future. The immediate priority for the ILO must be that of extending to the maximum degree possible, the scope, level and coverage of systems of social protection. This needs to be done in a way which is compatible with and supportive of economic development, particularly programmes of structural adjustment. Policies also need to take into account the existing constraints and realities, political and social as well as economic. But they must push the development of social security systems as far as these limits will allow. Inter alia this means:

- Within the limits of what is economically feasible, the promotion of tax-based systems of social protection to provide as full a basic coverage as possible for the population as whole, regardless of contribution history or acquired entitlements. This may require some review of budgetary priorities.

- The development and expansion of existing contributory social security mechanisms to ensure complete coverage of formal sector employees and their dependents, across the full range of social security contingencies, and where possible, to extend such coverage to the informal sector.

- The creation of space for the existence of supplementary and/or private sector schemes which complement, without detracting from, the universal basic provision or the social security based-schemes noted above.

- The creation of tripartite institutions and supervisory agencies for the proper coordination of the different means of providing social protection and for ensuring their long-term viability.

- The administrative and managerial reform of social security institutions to ensure greater operational efficiency, full compliance in the collection of contributions, and greater effectiveness in the disbursement of benefits.

- The promotion, in a normative context, of a greater sense of solidarity within systems of social protection and a greater willingness on the part of populations to enhance present measures of income redistribution.

4

Toward a cost-effective social security system[1]

George Kopits
Chief, Fiscal Operations Division
International Monetary Fund

The purpose of this paper is to trace in broad terms the root-causes and nature of the crisis faced by many social security systems — consisting of social insurance and social assistance schemes — around the world and to summarize the case for reforming them in the framework of economy-wide structural adjustment. Whereas there is clearly a need for complementing structural reform and stabilization with appropriate social safety nets,[2] there are equally compelling reasons for reforming entire social security systems — including such safety nets — as part of economy-wide adjustment programmes. The paper also examines the role of the International Monetary Fund (IMF) in enhancing the cost-effectiveness of social insurance and social assistance schemes. The closing section reviews the options and constraints faced in the design and implemen-

1. Comments by Jack Boorman, Ke-young Chu, Robert Hagemann, Stanford Ross, and Vito Tanzi are gratefully acknowledged. The views expressed do not necessarily represent those of the International Monetary Fund.

2. Broadly speaking, according to the definition adopted here, social safety nets encompass measures intended to alleviate directly the adverse effects of structural adjustment or various exogenous shocks on poverty. Thus, they include mainly social assistance schemes, but also certain insurance-type programmes such as unemployment compensation.

tation of cost-effective social security systems. The discussion is, of course, far from exhaustive, as it focuses mainly on cash benefits and financing issues in countries that are most in need of reform, namely, developing countries and post-socialist countries involved in market-oriented transition.

From promise and expansion to crisis

Over a period spanning nearly a century, earnings-related social insurance (mainly public pensions and unemployment compensation) and limited forms of social assistance were established first in Europe, followed in the Americas, and to a much lesser extent in other continents. Until the early 1970s, social insurance schemes – inspired mainly by the Bismarck model – prospered financially and gained considerable popularity, as the first generations of enrolled retirees and unemployed were able to benefit in amounts that often far exceeded their contributions during relatively short service periods.

Accumulated reserves of social security institutions were often used to finance government budget deficits, at practically no interest yield, with little regard for the long-term sustainability of the system. Also, reserves were earmarked to cross-subsidize health-care and other noncontributory schemes, or were invested in projects with a highly questionable rate of return. This approach seemed justifiable for partially funded defined-benefit-cum-defined-contribution programmes, given the continued expansion of the contributing workforce. In brief, the main preoccupation was the maximization of coverage of the enrolled population rather than with long-term financial stability and intergenerational equity. Whatever financing difficulties emerged, there was considerable scope for stepwise increases in payroll-based contribution rates.

Provision of social assistance, including health care, for the poor was rather uneven across countries. Traditionally, a more equitable income distribution was sought primarily through highly progressive personal income taxation and selected categorical subsidies. In many developing countries, price controls on key foodstuffs and other products deemed essential, as well as interest rate ceilings, proliferated on equity grounds. The accompanying subsidies were financed from general budget revenue.

It was largely the first oil shock that exposed the financial imbalances that underlay the social security programmes of many developing countries, in the context of severe macroeconomic disequilibria. Mounting inflationary pressures, rampant commodity shortages, external payments difficulties, increasing indebtedness, and a marked slowdown in growth, revealed major structural rigidities. Social security institutions were under financial stress. The real value of benefits was eroded by inflation, while new rounds of payroll tax rate hikes plus budgetary injections were needed to ensure financial solvency, in effect on a pay-as-you-go basis.[3]

These financial problems have been compounded by generous eligibility for benefits granted for political expediency rather than on the basis of either past contributions or genuine need. Potentially the most costly provision – often of a quasi-constitutional nature or enshrined formally in the constitution – is universal access to health care, with few or no qualifications. Excessive claims for sick pay, partial disability pensions, early retirement pensions, length-of-service pensions, and health-care benefits have been on the rise in a number of industrial countries and have placed an unsustainable burden on developing countries facing major macroeconomic imbalances. Meanwhile, the contribution base began to shrink partly because of a slowdown in real income growth in the formal sector. The rise in the benefit-contribution ratio has been exacerbated by the turnaround in demographic trends, driven by declining birth rates and rising life expectancy – albeit the full repercussions will not be felt in developing countries until the next century.[4] The typical policy response in many countries – sometimes as a conditioned reflex – has been to raise statutory contribution rates further.

These developments, along with a lack of transparency and accountability of social security finances (often combined with corrupt and inefficient administration), weakened the perception of any linkage between benefit eligibility and contribution record, and thus, undermined compliance with what has come to be regarded increasingly as an onerous form of regressive payroll taxation. In turn, incorporation of high payroll tax rates in labour costs contributed to the erosion in the taxing country's international competitiveness – absent border adjustment for payroll taxes, as provided for indirect taxes under the destination principle, in foreign trade – imposing yet an additional burden of adjustment on the exchange rate.

---

3. As only minimum benefits were indexed for inflation, many social insurance programmes approached de facto the Beveridge model which calls for flat means-tested benefits. Australia and New Zealand are among the few countries that adopted formally such a model.

4. A destabilizing aspect of these two sources of demographic change is that whereas the decline in birth rates has little immediate depressing effect on social security receipts, the rise in life expectancy tends to raise aggregate benefits in the short run. For an analysis of the implications of ageing for social security finances, see Hagemann and Nicoletti (1989). Whereas population ageing in industrial countries has been due mainly to reduced birth rates in recent decades ("ageing from the bottom"), increases in old-age dependency ratios in developing countries seem heavily influenced by increased life expectancy at all ages ("ageing from the top").

The social security crisis is nowhere more acute than in the post-socialist economies of Central and Eastern Europe and the former Soviet republics, resulting in the least adequate protection and the heaviest fiscal burden.[5] In addition to the above ailments, in these countries social security schemes have become grossly dysfunctional, owing to rigid ideological constraints. In the past, unemployment was hidden through large-scale redundancies in state-owned enterprises and through relatively easy eligibility for various social insurance benefits (especially low retirement age, generous sick pay and disability benefits), given the lack of unemployment compensation. The primary vehicle for poverty alleviation took the form of price subsidies to satisfy merit wants — available to all, regardless of need.

At present, during the market-oriented transition — even after the official recognition of unemployment and poverty and the creation of specific schemes to deal with them openly — the dysfunctional treatment of unemployment in most countries seems to have been aggravated with increased recourse to early retirement and disability benefits. At the same time, these countries are singularly incapable of delivering social assistance to the needy, lacking the necessary administrative capacity. The explanation lies largely in the fact that all social security programmes were run by state-owned enterprises, leaving some segments of the population entirely disenfranchised. As these enterprises become increasingly exposed to market discipline, relinquish their role of suppliers of social services and shed redundant labour, there is bound to be a rapid increase in poverty.

The case for reform

In an effort to correct macroeconomic imbalances, beginning in the late 1970s, a number of developing countries embarked on comprehensive adjustment programmes that, besides short-term stabilization, were aimed at bringing about structural reform. The latter consisted mainly of liberalization of commodity prices, interest rates and the exchange rate, financial and fiscal reform, overhaul or privatization of state-owned enterprises, and trade and payments liberalization.[6] It was recognized early on that both the magnitude and nature of such structural changes, in combination with fiscal and monetary restraint, could have a significant short-run adverse impact on incomes and employment.

---

5.   See Kopits (1992).

6.   For a recent overview of IMF-supported structural adjustment programmes, see Jafarey (1992).

Such an outcome is inherent in post-socialist economies undergoing market-oriented transformation.

Clearly, the removal of subsidies to loss-making public enterprises, phaseout of consumer subsidies to households, especially involving foodstuffs, could create a short-run deterioration of social conditions as compared to the former status quo. Arguably, however, under most adjustment programmes living conditions improved in comparison to the relevant counterfactual situation — characterized by widespread shortages, hoarding, falling real incomes, black market activities — which was unsustainable given domestic financial disinter-mediation, output contraction and capital flight.[7] Moreover, market-oriented structural reform combined with stabilization would lead to sustainable economic growth in the medium term.

Beginning in the second half of the 1980s, the Fund sought to deal with the social consequences of adjustment programmes in an active and systematic manner. In essence, the underlying rationale was the necessity to buttress the social and political acceptance of the adjustment effort with an explicit effort to contain adverse short-run distributional implications. As part of its appraisal of macroeconomic policies, whether in the context of Article IV consultations or of adjustment programmes, the IMF staff began to examine the possible consequences of the stance and mix of key adjustment measures on socioeconomic conditions in member countries, and to identify ways of strengthening the social safety net for adversely affected groups. This initiative focused primarily on easing the temporary impact of such measures on the poorest strata in low-income countries.[8]

More recently, increasing attention has been paid to comprehensive social security reform in the framework of structural adjustment. At the request of member countries, the IMF provides technical assistance to support such reform. Since 1989, more than a dozen member countries received assistance in the design and administration of social security schemes (especially public pensions, unemployment compensation, health care, and social assistance).[9] In

---

7. In Turkey, for example, there was evidence of increases in net real wages and nonagricultural employment under one of the largest IMF-supported structural adjustment programmes in the first half of the 1980s. See Kopits (1987).

8. For a discussion of the IMF's role in poverty alleviation, see International Monetary Fund (1990).

9. Countries that received such assistance include Algeria, Bolivia, Brazil, Bulgaria, Greece, Hungary, Indonesia, and most former Soviet republics. The technical assistance report on Hungary — the first one prepared by an IMF mission in the social security area, including social safety nets — is scheduled for publication shortly.

addition, social security reform measures, along with other structural fiscal reform measures, have been increasingly incorporated in IMF-supported adjustment programmes.

Reform options and constraints

The main goal of social security reform is cost-effectiveness — meaning "the biggest *social* bang for the *fiscal* buck" — based on the premise that social security can no longer be viewed simply in terms of magnitude and coverage of benefits, but must be assessed also in terms of fiscal and allocative costs. In other words, a cost-effective social security system provides maximum protection at the least cost in terms of fiscal resources and allocative distortions, and does not contribute to a macroeconomic imbalance. This fundamental criterion for reform encompasses a range of considerations, with implications for the design and implementation of the system. More specifically, it allows for a variety of reform options while being subject to a number of limiting constraints.

In the first place, it is necessary to take into account explicitly cultural and social characteristics, as well as historical antecedents, of each country. Obviously, these characteristics shape behaviour, attitudes and aspirations with regard to the provision of social services. At one end of the spectrum, there are societies where the extended family or village structure operates relatively well as an informal social security scheme, obviating the urgent introduction of large-scale public pensions and assistance schemes. Such behaviour permits, for instance, the grafting of Health Maintenance Organizations (HMOs), perhaps with some government support, as an efficient form of health-care insurance. The example of certain Asian countries (such as Indonesia, under the *goton royong* principle), and to a lesser extent, Mediterranean countries, illustrates this approach. At the other end, in countries where households have been atomized and informal self-help arrangements have been weakened or broken, there is an immediate need to provide an extended safety net. This is the case, for instance, in much of the former Soviet Union, where the individual (cast in the mold of a *homo sovieticus)* has been made totally dependent on the state, through his or her workplace — often with insurmountable barriers to mobility.

A second consideration requires that social security programmes do not interfere with the efficient allocation of resources and do not act as a disincentive to work and to save. For the sake of allocative efficiency, administrative simplicity, and increased labour mobility, social security provisions should be uniform across occupations and economic activities, including the government workforce. Unless justified by clearly differentiated risk (under a defined-benefit regime), eligibility for benefits, benefit levels, contribution rates, and the degree of subsidization, if any, should be uniform. Moreover, social insurance schemes (including Chilean-type government-mandated private pension funds) can be supplemented usefully with voluntary private insurance and retirement funds. Such profit-oriented private schemes, if appropriately regulated to protect the interests of enrollees, can become an effective vehicle for further development of financial markets and for raising the saving propensities of households.[10] In addition, nongovernment initiatives – by charitable, religious, or other organizations – that provide valuable assistance to the needy, deserve support. Nevertheless, the provision of tax or regulatory preferences for private insurance, retirement and assistance must be weighed against broader considerations of tax policy design and revenue needs.

A third and related consideration is the need to calibrate the social security system to a given country's level of economic development and labour market conditions. To promote labour force participation in the formal sector, it is necessary to remove impediments and disincentives to employment in that sector. To be specific, besides strengthening the linkage between benefits and wage-based contributions, contribution rates should be kept relatively low in a low-wage, labour surplus economy. The structure and level of contributions and other forms of financing must be consistent with the overall tax system. Furthermore, a low level of development and a large labour surplus render difficult the provision of means-tested flat pensions and other benefits in many developing economies.

As a corollary to the above considerations, it cannot be overemphasized that social security reform should be geared to the eradication of excess consumption and waste of scarce resources. With few exceptions,[11] open-ended consumer price subsidies should be replaced with means-tested transfers. Given administrative limitations, such as those prevailing in some developing or post-socialist economies, it may be necessary to resort to various forms of categorical transfers to well-identified groups (for instance, households with young children and the elderly), possibly in the form of benefits in kind. Also, automatic indexation of benefits is fully justified for equity reasons.[12] Health-

---

10. For a primer on the regulatory framework for private pension funds, see Guérard and Jenkins (1993).

11. For instance, subsidization of passenger mass transport is warranted on environmental grounds and as a means to reduce congestion costs.

12. Selection of an appropriate basis for benefit indexation depends on the equity standard chosen: consumer price index, minimum subsistence price index, or index of net earnings. However, compensation for a one-off adjustment of relative prices may require a different yardstick of adjustment.

care provision is another area of considerable potential for saving through various cost-containment techniques. In particular, stepped-up preventive practices and education, increased information about medical and hospital costs for both health-care users and providers, user fees and supply incentives, should reduce abuse and waste.

An additional consideration involves the need for a clear institutional distinction among social security schemes by function or purpose: retirement, disability and survivors' pensions, unemployment compensation, health care and poverty alleviation. Separation of social insurance programmes and social assistance programmes, notwithstanding some inevitable overlaps, helps to differentiate their characteristics, so that the public may better understand the purpose of each programme, and to promote accountability for each programme. Such a functional distinction implies that public pensions should not be used to alleviate unemployment — through a low retirement age or easy access to early retirement benefits and partial disability benefits. This differentiation also has implications for the sources of financing. Social insurance programmes (old-age, disability, unemployment) are to be financed primarily with wage-based contributions by the insured employee and by the employer on his or her behalf, supplemented by income from any invested reserves created with such contributions. Further, it is necessary to establish a close relationship between insurance-type benefits and contributions so as to gain acceptance and support for such programmes in the labour force — a critical element for their success. Such an approach does not preclude a redistributive element, for instance, in the form of a floor and a ceiling on pensions. By contrast, the main source of financing social assistance schemes should be general tax revenue.

Fifth, attention must be devoted to an important intertemporal consideration that is often neglected owing to political expediency or preoccupation strictly with short-term macroeconomic disequilibria. Besides ensuring social protection and fairness for the present generation, social security must seek an equitable distribution of benefits and costs between present and future generations. Public pension programmes, in particular, should be financially self-sustaining over long periods of time, capable of withstanding considerable demographic and economic fluctuations. Viewed as an intergenerational contractual obligation — to be honoured notwithstanding a change in government or in regime — a public retirement scheme commits future generations that do not have an opportunity to influence or vote on the design of the system, to support the present generation. An overly generous benefit structure, despite the associated fiscal burden and allocative distortions, inherited from the past, usually can be corrected only through a gradual and painful reform, including costly grandfathering of existing benefits, following a protracted national debate.

Finally, it is imperative to observe certain constraints on the speed and scope of implementation of reform. The size of the formal sector, quite apart from the effects of social security thereon, imposes an outer limit on the coverage of insurance-type programmes. The capacity to administer the collection of contributions and the disbursement of benefits imposes an even tighter limit in the short run. Although not bound to the formal sector, the delivery of social assistance is determined chiefly by fiscal resources and administrative capacity. Equally important for the success of the reform, especially against a record of unfulfilled expectations, is the institutional transparency of social security operations and accountability of management. In this respect, the creation of well-administered public trust funds — one for each social insurance programme — can make an important contribution to credibility and popular acceptance. An overarching constraint, particularly on health-care and social assistance programmes, as well as on the extent of grandfathering during the transition to a new system, is the availability of fiscal resources. Failure to observe any one of these critical constraints is bound to undermine the integrity and credibility of the system from the very outset. Accordingly, the task of overhauling the institutional and administrative framework should be assigned high priority in the reform effort. In addition, it is important to the establishment of viable institutions that legally prescribed programmes be simple and transparent enough to be administered in accordance with their terms.

References

Guérard, Y.; Jenkins, G. 1993. *Building Private Pension Systems: A Handbook*. San Francisco, International Center for Economic Growth.

Hagemann, R.; Nicoletti, G. 1989. "Ageing Populations: Economic Effects and Implications for Public Finance". *OECD Economic Studies*. Spring. pp. 51-96.

International Monetary Fund. 1990. "The Fund and Poverty Issues: A Progress Report" in *Development Issues*. Developing Committee Pamphlet No. 26. Washington, September 24. pp. 29-34.

Jafarey, V.A. (moderator). 1992. *Structural Adjustment and Macroeconomic Policy Issues* Washington, International Monetary Fund and Pakistan Administrative Staff College.

Kopits, G. 1987. *Structural Reform, Stabilization, and Growth in Turkey*. Occasional Paper 52, Washington, International Monetary Fund.

Kopits, G. 1992. "Social Security" in *Fiscal Policies in Economies in Transition*. Edited by V. Tanzi. Washington, International Monetary Fund. pp. 291-311.

5

Swiss Chilanpore
The way forward for pension reform?

Dimitri Vittas
Senior Financial Specialist
Country Economics Department
World Bank

Many countries around the world are contemplating far-reaching reforms of their pension systems. In Europe, Italy and Greece are confronted with a financial crisis of their public pension system and suffer from highly fragmented private or semi-private sectors. Other OECD countries are faced with growing demographic pressures that put a question mark on the longterm sustainability of their pension systems. In Britain, massive fraud in the pension scheme of one large company group has endangered the occupational pensions of large numbers of workers, while in the United States extensive underfunding of a good number of large company-based pension schemes is putting a big strain on the finances of the Pension Benefits Guaranty Corporation. In Eastern Europe, the pension systems are unable to cope with the macroeconomic shocks afflicting these countries and have effectively reneged on their promises for overgenerous and unsustainable pensions. In Latin America, several countries are considering a fundamental reform away from unfunded defined benefit systems and toward structures that comprise as an important element fully funded schemes based on individual accounts. At the same time, countries in Anglophone Africa and Asia are moving away from national provident funds and toward defined benefit social insurance systems.

Given all this commotion and interest for reform, a basic question can be raised: Is there a blueprint for pension reform? Are there lessons from the experience of different countries that could be combined in laying down what could be described as best practice in creating a new structure for the pension systems of different countries? The purpose of this paper is to bring together the experience of three countries with relatively successful economies and pension systems. It puts forward a suggestion for the structure of a pension system that is dubbed Swiss Chilanpore. But before describing what Swiss Chilanpore is, it is important to make three basic points about pension systems and pension finance.

Point Number One: There is no perfect pension system. Funded or unfunded, private or public, defined benefit or defined contribution, redistributive or not, there is no system that can escape from the problems of moral hazard, adverse selection, agency costs and free riding. These afflict all types of financial and social contracts, but are especially acute in the case of pension contracts that span a period of 60 years or more.

Point Number Two: All pension systems require good government and good management to function well and to have any hope of accomplishing their objectives. A country that is deemed unable to run well a funded or unfunded public pension system, because of administrative inefficiency, shortage of skilled personnel, or political interference, would most likely also be unable to regulate and supervise a private pension system. Conversely, a country that can effectively regulate and supervise a private pension system can also run reasonably well a public pension system.

Point Number Three: All pension systems have to cope with the uncertainty that characterizes human existence and the simple, but inescapable, fact that we do not know the future. (These days we hardly know the present and we strongly dispute the past, but this is a different story.) All systems are exposed to the vagaries of macroeconomic imbalances, the peculiarities and unpredictability of fundamental demographic trends, and the implications of changes in the relative scarcity of labour and capital.

It is because all systems are imperfect, all require good governance, and all suffer from the effects of long-term uncertainty that a strong case can be made for establishing mixed pension systems. Swiss Chilanpore is such a mixed system. It is not a new type of Swiss cheese, but in the best traditions of good cheese-making, it combines contrasting features that bring out the best of its ingredients. A Swiss Chilanpore pension system would be based on the pension systems of three countries, Switzerland, Chile and Singapore, and would blend the hardheaded softness of the Swiss, the expensive yields of the Chilean scheme, and the ruthless efficiency of Singapore.

Similarities and differencies

These three countries have a number of features in common, but they also exhibit some important differences. The first similarity is that they all have compulsory systems that cover nearly every worker, except self-employed people. The second similarity is that they rely to a substantial degree on funded schemes. The financial resources accumulated in pension funds are large in relation to national income in all three countries. The third similarity is that they represent relatively successful economies with high levels of national and household saving. This is particularly so in the case of Singapore and Switzerland. Chile has suffered from the high inflation that has long characterized most Latin American countries. But allowing for the negative effect of high and volatile inflation on national saving, especially on financial savings, the financial performance of the Chilean pension funds has been quite remarkable.

Of course, several other countries exhibit characteristics similar to those of these three countries. For instance, Britain and the US have large funded pension schemes, though unlike Switzerland, employers in these countries are not compelled to offer pension schemes to all their employees. In Britain and the US less than half of private sector employees are covered by company pension schemes, against 100 per cent in Switzerland. Korea, India, China, Italy, Greece and other countries have high rates of household saving, but they do not have compulsory funded pension schemes. Finally, France and, perhaps to a lesser degree, Germany impose compulsory participation in pension schemes on their residents, but these schemes are not based on funded pension plans.

As already remarked, the three countries also exhibit some important differences. The Swiss system, like those of most OECD countries, is extremely complex and opaque. Although it is often referred to as a three-pillar system, it is in fact more like those modem American houses that are known as split-level contemporaries. The complexity of the system makes it difficult to measure its cost or to assess the investment performance of the funded components of the system.

For its part, the Singaporean system is quite simple and, as will be argued below, operationally very efficient. However, it suffers from lack of transparency and produces relatively low returns and benefits to its affiliates.

The Chilean system is very simple and highly transparent and is also supported by very effective regulation and supervision. It has produced very high real returns, but suffers from very high operating costs. These afflict not only the pension system itself but also the private annuity market on which it is partly based.

Unlike Switzerland, neither Chile nor Singapore incorporate in their pension systems intentional redistribution in favour of low income workers. On the contrary, both may inadvertently cause unintentional redistribution that may be perverse by penalizing low income workers. Nevertheless, both countries offer some forms of minimum pensions.

The Swiss system

The Swiss pension system is typically described as a three-pillar system. The "first pillar" is a social insurance scheme that pays defined basic benefits, the "second pillar" consists of the compulsory company-based plans that pay complementary pensions aiming to achieve a satisfactory replacement rate, and the "third pillar" consists of voluntary savings, including fiscally supported pension plans for self-employed people and other workers not covered by company schemes. But, as already noted, the Swiss system is in reality a five level split system with two of its pillars split into smaller and uneven parts.

The first pillar is a defined benefit plan and is divided into two parts: the first has a redistributive objective and pays a minimum flat rate pension given by a base index that amounted in 1990 to 800 Swiss francs per month or about 20 per cent of average earnings; the second part pays an earnings-related pension equal to an additional 20 per cent of earnings, subject to a limit that the total social pension cannot be higher than twice the annual base index. Thus, the maximum social pension does not exceed 40 per cent of average earnings. The second part has an intergenerational insurance objective, ensuring a replacement rate of at least 40 per cent of lifetime earnings for average workers, irrespective of the investment performance of the funded pillars of the system.

The earnings-related part of the pension is based on revalued (actualized) average lifetime annual earnings, while the flat rate part is proportionately adjusted to the length of a person's career. Actualization of lifetime earnings is based on the wage index.

The Swiss social pension system is redistributive in favour of low income workers. In theory, it can achieve a replacement rate of over 100 per cent for workers earning less than 25 per cent of average earnings. The replacement rate falls to 40 per cent for workers with average earnings and to 20 per cent for workers with twice average earnings. In practice, replacement rates are affected by the revaluation factors used by the social security system and by the length of a worker's career.

The Swiss "first pillar" is a pay-as-you-go system, financed with a total contribution rate of 8.4 per cent, equally divided between employers and employees. In addition, the state makes a contribution from general revenue to cover 20 per cent of pension payments. Social pensions used to be indexed to prices, but since 1980 pensions in payment are indexed to the arithmetic mean of the wage and consumer price indices. Adjustment is made every two years or when the index increases cumulatively by over 8 per cent.

Because it is based on actualized lifetime earnings and is adjusted for the length of a person's career, the Swiss social pension system avoids the problems that bedevil so many developing countries. These provisions weaken the incentive to misreport (understate or overstate) earnings during a worker's career. They also discourage moral hazard since workers will not be entitled to the minimum pension by participating in the scheme only for a minimum vesting period. OECD estimates indicate that the internal rate of return in the Swiss system is higher for low than for high income workers, which is in line with the intentions of the designers of the system (OECD 1988). The social pension system does not appear to suffer from extensive capricious or perverse redistribution.

Perhaps because of the proportionality of social pensions, many old age Swiss residents receive pensions that are inadequate for maintaining an acceptable minimum standard of living. The Swiss authorities have been forced to introduce a supplementary pension payable to old persons with insufficient means. This effectively represents a social assistance pension, funded from general budget revenues. In the terminology of a multi-pillar or split level structure, it amounts to an annex or an extension that is attached to the first pillar.

The "second pillar" is based on company pension schemes, the offer of which is compulsory since the enactment of the law on professional pensions in 1985. This law implemented the constitutional amendment on pensions that was first voted by the Swiss public in 1972. There is considerable uncertainty as to whether the second pillar is a defined contribution or defined benefit scheme. In theory, the law specifies some minimum provisions which relate to the contributions that need to be paid each year. These take into account some targeted level of replacement rate, but employers do not appear to be required to make up any shortfall that may arise because of insufficient investment returns, except that they have to credit each retirement account with interest at a minimum (nominal) rate of 4 per cent. Thus, if the nominal return is less than 4 per cent, employers are presumably forced to make up the difference.

The target replacement rate seems to be an integrated pension of 60 per cent of final salary, though many large employers, especially in industry and finance, aim for 70 per cent or more. These employers appear to offer defined benefit plans and to be prepared to make up any shortfall on investment performance. These schemes can in theory at least be seen as a separate part of the second pillar and to add credence to the argument made above about the split level nature of the Swiss system.

The constitutional amendment of 1972 and the implementing law of 1985 did not have as large an impact on the provision of company pensions as might appear at first sight. This is because most large and medium size employers have long operated pension schemes for their employees. The new law has had a much bigger impact on small employers, who have tended to set up contracts with insurance companies and commercial banks.

The law specifies that the contribution rate should vary by age and sex and should be divided equally between employers and employees. The rate starts at 7 per cent for young male workers between 25 and 34, rises to 10 per cent for those between 35 and 44, 15 per cent for those between 45 and 54, and 18 per cent for those between 55 and 65, which is the normal retirement age for males. The rates are the same for female workers except that the higher rates apply respectively after age 32, 42 and 52. The normal retirement age for women is 62. Contributions must be made on covered earnings, which are given by the difference between the annual base index and up to six times that level. Employers are of course free to cover earnings in excess of these limits and to offer defined benefit pensions.

Employers are required either to establish separate legal entities, often in the form of foundations for these pension schemes, or to entrust their insurance and management with financial institutions, such as insurance companies and commercial banks.

The investment performance of pension funds has not received as much attention as, for instance in Chile or in Britain. Although there are investment rules placing maximum limits on different types of assets, there are no requirements for minimum (absolute or relative) investment returns. In fact, despite the private management of the funds and the benefits of competition, the real rates of return have on average been very mediocre. Investing institutions appear to have emphasized safety at the expense of return.

Detailed data on the investment performance of private pension funds are not readily available. Estimates based on macrodata and on the known asset distribution of the portfolios of the pension funds suggest that the average annual real rate of return over the past quarter of a century amounted to 1.5 per cent (Davis 1992). This was lower than the average annual growth rate of real wages which was 3.2 per cent (the highest among the more advanced OECD countries). Thus, the negative gap between the real rate of return and the growth rate of real wages was quite significant at 1.7 per cent. In recent years, there has been an attempt to improve on the investment record of the pension funds as both insurance companies and commercial banks have started to compete more aggressively, to shift their investment policies towards domestic and foreign equities, and to stress investment performance in their publicity material.

Although most company schemes are effectively defined contribution plans, they appear to suffer from vesting and portability problems. Swiss law requires immediate vesting for employee contributions, but partial vesting after 5 years of service and full vesting after 30 years for employer contributions. The law is unclear about vesting rights with regard to accumulated investment income.

The portability of funds is the subject of much controversy. Funds can be transferred to the pension system of the new employer or they can be used to purchase a restricted insurance policy from an insurance company or to open a restricted account with a bank. However, the calculation of the pension rights to be transferred raises issues of actuarial fairness that are difficult to resolve.

Final salary defined benefit plans of the "second pillar" also favour high fliers (especially managers who get promoted and receive big salary increases late in their career) at the expense of slow plodders. Thus, company pension schemes may give rise to perverse redistribution from early leavers to long stayers as well as from slow plodders to high fliers. In addition, unintentional redistribution may occur by significant variations in real rates of return for members of defined contribution plans. A guarantee fund, financed by premiums assessed on covered wages, insures workers against insolvency of the pension foundations set up by employers.

The "third pillar" consists of voluntary savings in the form of bank deposits, insurance policies, other financial assets, or real assets such as housing. In this pillar, an important part is played by personal pension plans for self employed people and other workers not covered by company schemes. These plans, as well as additional voluntary arrangements for old age pensions, are supported by favourable tax treatment.

Contributions to the social, compulsory company and voluntary pension systems (up to specified limits) are tax deductible, as is all investment income. Thus, unlike other OECD countries, the tax treatment in Switzerland does not discriminate against the social system. Moreover, the government contribution to the first pillar may be justified as an attempt to equalize the fiscal benefits across pillars. Pension benefits are generally subject to income tax.

Because of the complexity and opaqueness of the system, it is not easy to calculate its total operating costs and the required total contribution rate for achieving targeted pensions. Estimates by consulting actuaries indicate that a full career worker with a salary equivalent to average earnings would receive a pension equal to 54 per cent of pre-retirement pay at a total contribution rate of 12.3 per cent, of which 7 per cent is paid by the employer and 5.3 per cent by the employee (Wyatt 1990). However, this contribution rate appears quite low by comparison to the rate of 8.4 per cent for the first pillar and the rates ranging between 7 per cent and 18 per cent imposed by the law on professional pensions.

In summary, the first pillar, supported by its annex, appears to achieve well its redistributive and insurance objectives and does not seem to be exceedingly costly. But the second and third pillars are highly complex and opaque, with little attention being paid on investment performance and administrative efficiency. A considerable amount of unintentional and for the most part rather perverse redistribution appears to be taking place in the second pillar.

The Singaporean system

The pension system of Singapore is organized on national provident fund principles. All workers, except self-employed people, are required to participate in the Central Provident Fund (CPF). The CPF is a public agency that administers the system, collects contributions, keeps records, pays out benefits, and invests the accumulated funds. The last-named function is very simple for the CPF since nearly all the funds are invested in government instruments. The investment decisions that matter are taken by two other very important government institutions, the Monetary Authority of Singapore (MAS) and the Government of Singapore Investment Corporation (GSIC).

The CPF was first established in 1955 after a long debate that appeared to favour the creation of a social insurance system, but was overruled by the London Colonial Office (Queisser 1991). Contribution rates were initially quite low, no more than 10 per cent divided equally between employers and employees. The system was a pure mandatory retirement savings scheme, forcing workers to save for their old age and allowing lump sum withdrawals on reaching age 55.

Contribution rates were raised to 13 per cent in 1968 when a decision was also made to allow interim, but controlled, withdrawals for the purchase of houses. Since then, there have been several increases in contribution rates, which reached a staggering total of 50 per cent in 1984. Subsequently, however, because of the negative impact on employment creation during the recession of 1985/6, the total contribution rate was lowered to 35 per cent by setting the employer's rate to 10 per cent (Vittas and Skully 1991). More recently, the contribution rate has stabilized at the still very high level of 40 per cent, with a long-term aim to divide this equally between employers and employees. Because contributions are divided equally between employers and employees, this corresponds to an effective rate of 33 per cent, since contributions of 40 are paid out of total payroll of 120. An innovation of recent years is the institution of lower contribution rates for people aged over 55, while from the very beginning workers earning less than a specified minimum were exempt from making contributions.

Over the years, additional investment opportunities for investments in approved securities and for spending for education were allowed, while health insurance was also included among the benefits of the system. Also, since 1987, workers are required to keep a minimum sum in their account after reaching 55. This is fixed by the CPF and is adequate to purchase on retirement at age 60 a minimum life annuity equal to about 25 per cent of average earnings.

The CPF is a defined contribution system with no intentional redistribution. Its primary objective is a forced saving one for old age. These days it is not a purely retirement savings scheme since it allows use of funds for several other purposes. Thus, its secondary objective is to encourage spending on merit goods (health, housing, education). Although redistribution is not among its objectives, it is often argued that the CPF creates perverse redistribution because of the low rates of interest credited on account balances. This is particularly so because only high income workers can avail themselves of the opportunities to invest in other approved but high yielding assets (Asher 1991).

Although the CPF is a mono-pillar system, the Government of Singapore operates a public assistance pension scheme that offers to destitute old people a small pension that is half the size of the minimum pension imposed under the CPF and amounts to about 12 per cent of average earnings.

One of the strengths of the CPF is its high efficiency and very low operating costs. In 1990, total operating costs, including depreciation provisions, amounted to 0.53 per cent of annual contributions, 0.21 per cent of wages and

0.10 per cent of accumulated assets (CPF 1990). These ratios are very low by international standards and compare very favourably with those achieved by large employer-based company schemes in Britain and the US. For instance, Postel, the company managing the pension funds for the employees of British Telecom and the British Post Office, has total operating and investment management costs of 0.1 per cent or 10 basis points of total assets. This is divided between 6 basis points for operating costs and 4 basis points for investment management costs.

Apart from the lack of redistributive objectives, two fundamental weaknesses of the CPF are its very high total contribution rate and the low rate of interest credited on account balances. The latter has fluctuated over the years but appears to have averaged around 2 per cent in real terms between 1960 and 1990 (Table 1). Since 1987, the CPF rate of interest has been linked to the average of the rate on savings deposits and the rate on 12-month fixed time deposits with banks. In view of the long-term and contractual nature of CPF balances, a higher rate would appear more appropriate. Given a growth rate of real wages of over 4 per cent, the real rate of return appears low to secure a high replacement rate, despite the very high contribution rate. For instance, when pensions are indexed to prices, working life is 40 years, retirement life (with an allowance for survivor pensions) is 20 years, a contribution rate of at least 25 per cent may be required to achieve a replacement ratio of 43 per cent of final earnings, when the growth rate of real wages is 4 per cent and the real rate of return is 2 per cent (Vittas 1992, Schwarz 1992). In Singapore, the effective contribution rate is 33 per cent, but a substantial part of savings is used for investments in housing and other assets as well as for the purpose of financing education. Some of these assets could provide economic support in retirement, though it is clear that not all CPF savings would be available. Moreover, it should be noted that even with a low replacement rate, the absolute level of the pension would be quite high as a result of the high growth rate of real wages.

It is not easy to understand why the CPF rate of interest is low although, unlike most other national provident funds, it has on average been positive in real terms. Nevertheless, Malaysia which has also long operated a national provident fund has been able to pay a higher real rate of interest than the Singaporean CPF (Table 2).

Table 1   *Central Provident Fund of Singapore*
             Nominal and Real Rates of Interest

	1960s	1970s	1980s	1960-90
Nominal Rate	4.62	6.20	5.27	5.36
Inflation (CPI)	1.09	6.45	2.35	3.27
Real Rate	3.50	-0.24	2.86	2.02

One explanation for the low rate of interest is that this is what members prefer because the rate of interest on mortgage loans from the Housing Development Board is also linked to the same index. However, a low mortgage rate favours high income employees and also encourages excessive investment in housing. In Singapore, it is claimed that over 90 per cent of people are owner occupiers, an impressive achievement on the face of it. But the ratio of house prices to annual income appears to be near or even above 10. By comparison, the house price to income ratio in the US is less than 3. This implies a very high price for the privilege of owner occupation in Singapore. Part of this may be explained by the shortage of land, but the heavy demand for owner occupied housing, supported by the forced savings scheme of the CPF, may also be a factor.

Table 2   *Employees Provident Fund of Malaysia*
             Nominal and Real Rates of Interest

	1960s	1970s	1980s	1960-90
Nominal Rate	5.20	6.69	8.25	6.71
Inflation	0.91	5.89	3.27	3.34
Real Rate	4.25	0.75	4.82	3.26

A second explanation for the low interest rate is that this represents official policy that accumulates hidden reserves for the future needs of the Singaporean economy, an economy that is otherwise without natural resources. The CPF invests nearly all its funds in specially issued and nontradable government bonds and in liquid deposit balances placed with MAS. These funds are not used for domestic investment purposes but are part of the massive foreign exchange reserves of Singapore. As is well known, Singapore has by far the highest level of foreign exchange reserves on a per capita basis. It is claimed, though no statistics are published, that very high real returns have been realized on foreign assets, especially by GSIC, which invests in foreign equities in perhaps a similar fashion to the Kuwait Investment Office (KIO). There is no reason to doubt these claims although, because of the complete lack of transparency and publicity, it is also impossible to corroborate them.

To summarize, the Singaporean pension system is a defined contribution scheme with a very high contribution rate and a rather modest but positive real rate of return on accumulated balances. It is characterized by very low operating costs and by the build-up of massive hidden reserves through the accumulation of allegedly high yielding foreign exchange assets. The system does not have redistributive objectives, though a very modest public assistance pension is paid to destitute old people and some unintentional but perverse redistribution may take place. Its main objectives are forced saving for old age and spending on merit goods.

The Chilean system

The new Chilean system was introduced in 1981. It is a mandatory retirement savings scheme that was created to replace an insolvent social pension system that operated on a "pay-as-you-go" basis. The scheme requires all employees to contribute 10 per cent of their earnings until their normal retirement age, which is 65 for men and 60 for women. No contribution is imposed on employers, although they are required to withhold employee contributions and transfer them to the account holding companies. On retirement, workers must either purchase a life annuity from an insurance company or arrange a schedule of programmed withdrawals from their account. Lump sum payments are allowed only if account balances exceed the sum required to purchase an annuity equal to 70 per cent of final pay.

Like the Singaporean CPF, the Chilean system is a defined contribution system based on individual capitalization accounts, where pension benefits depend on the contributions made over a person's working career and the investment income earned on accumulated balances. Workers are required to purchase term life and disability insurance and to pay an additional commission to cover the premiums for these insurance policies as well as the operating costs of the system.

The Chilean system has some unique characteristics. It is government mandated and regulated, but completely privately managed by a number of authorized pension management companies, known as *Administradoras de Fondos de Pensiones* or AFPS. To ensure simplicity and transparency, regulations impose a strict limit of "one account per worker" and "one pension fund per AFP" (Vittas and Iglesias 1992). Affiliates receive regular statements with information about the credited contributions and the investment income of their fund.

To ensure the solvency of the system, the pension funds are legally separated from the management companies. Strict rules are imposed on AFPS, both regarding their capital reserves, the investment of pension fund assets, and their performance relative to the average for the AFP industry as a whole. Investment rules emphasize safety and profitability. A certain amount of diversification is required and for this purpose maximum limits are imposed on portfolio shares in different classes of instruments as well as in instruments of different issuers. No attempt is made to direct the investment of funds in high priority economic or social projects. The system is subject to strict, even draconian, regulation and to very close and effective supervision.

A very important feature of the system is the individual choice granted to affiliates to transfer their accounts between AFPS. Individual choice is expected to maintain pressure on AFPs to compete and operate efficiently, though experience has shown that unlimited choice to transfer accounts may result in very high operating costs, mostly because of publicity and marketing expenses and the actual account switching costs. Individual choice in the purchase of annuities has also given rise to high publicity and selling costs.

During the first ten years of its operation, the AFP has been remarkably successful. The annual real rate of return on pension fund assets has averaged over 13 per cent and total balances reached nearly 30 per cent of national income. Although this impressive performance of the AFP system is the result of the economic recovery of the Chilean economy and is linked first to the rise in real interest rates and then to their substantial fall, there is little doubt that, but for the existence of the AFP system, the vast majority of Chilean workers would not have been able to partake in the high investment returns and remarkable appreciation of capital values of the late 1980s.

As a defined contribution system, the Chilean system is ostensibly a mono-pillar system with no intentional redistribution. Some redistribution may take place, however, through the government guarantee that workers with at least 20 years of contributions will always receive the minimum pension. It is not clear how many workers will benefit from this guarantee. Clearly, this depends on the future relationship between wage growth and real returns.

Estimates put the proportion of workers that might benefit to between 40 per cent and 50 per cent (Gillion and Bonilla 1992), though the burden on the government may be rather small given that it will only have to make up for the shortfall between a worker's AFP pension and the minimum pension. Some estimates put this burden at no more than 1 per cent of GDP, though these calculations are extremely sensitive to assumptions regarding the values of basic parameters (Schwarz and Vittas 1992). The Government of Chile also pays minimum pensions to destitute old persons, but the number of potential beneficiaries appears to be small and eligibility is subject to strict means testing.

In addition to the guarantee regarding minimum pensions, the authorities impose on AFPs, and guarantee in case of AFP failure, a minimum investment return relative to the average for all pension funds. The government also guarantees, subject to specified limits, the value of life annuities with insurance companies.

Some features of the Chilean scheme give rise to regressive redistribution in favour of high income workers. This arises from two main sources. First, because the structure of commission charges includes both a flat fee and a per valorem fee, low income workers are effectively credited with a much lower rate of return than high income workers. Data for the first ten years of the AFP system show that low income workers obtained a real rate of return of 7.5 per cent against 10.5 per cent for high income workers and 13 per cent for the totality of the pension fund (Vittas and Iglesias 1992). The difference is caused by the imposition of the flat fee, which in the initial years of the scheme was quite high, but which has declined significantly in real terms. In fact, several AFPs have now abolished their flat fees altogether. Unintentional redistribution may also arise from variations in returns among AFPs, though these are limited by the required minimum relative investment returns on pension funds.

The second perverse redistribution arises from the forced use of annuities. In theory, life annuities should take account of the shorter life expectancy of poorer people or people from particularly arduous occupations. In practice, however, it seems that low income workers, not only do not benefit from lower annuity prices, but may also pay much higher commission charges for their life annuities than high income workers. The extent of perverse redistribution through the use of life annuities is not known, but appears to give rise to concern among Chilean policy makers and analysts.

Another point of concern is the high level of operating costs. Operating costs charged on affiliates, after deducting the premiums paid for term life and disability insurance, amount on average to 15.4 per cent of annual contributions, 1.54 per cent of wages, and 2.3 per cent of total assets. A comparison of the experience of Singapore and Chile shows that, depending on which ratio is used, the Chilean system was 29, 7 and 23 times more expensive than the Singaporean scheme. Operating costs in Chile are higher than those of the Employees Provident Fund in Malaysia, although they are much smaller than those of the Zambian National Provident Fund (Table 3).

Two of these three ratios can be very misleading. First, the ratio of operating costs to contributions is distorted by the size of the contribution rate. Given that most expenses of a pension system depend on the number of affiliates and are insensitive to the size of the contributions, a country with a high contribution rate will tend to report a low ratio of operating costs to contributions, and vice versa. Singapore with a contribution rate of 40 per cent of nominal wages has a much higher flow of annual contributions than Chile where the contribution rate is only 10 per cent. Malaysia had a nominal contribution rate of 20 per cent in 1989 (raised to 22 per cent in 1992), while the Zambian rate was 10 per cent. Second, the ratio of operating costs to total assets is affected by the age and maturity of the system. A mature system with a large accumulation of balances will tend to report a lower cost to assets ratio. In contrast, the third ratio, the ratio of operating costs to annual wages, is unaffected by these distortions and is perhaps the most relevant for comparing operating efficiency. This still shows the Chilean system to be seven times more expensive than the Singaporean one.

Operating costs are high in Chile for two main reasons. First, computerization is much less advanced than in Singapore and there is considerable duplication in both computer systems and branch networks for the collection of contributions and payment of pensions. Second, expenditure on publicity and advertising is quite high in order to encourage switching between AFPs. Because of the lack of a central computer and clearing system, account switching costs are not insignificant. Although often overlooked, account switching also imposes heavy costs on employers, who are required to withhold contributions from payroll and pay them over to individual AFPs according to the choice of their workers. High marketing costs also bedevil the life annuity market. The Chilean authorities are considering various measures to reduce operating costs. These include restrictions on the frequency of the right to transfer accounts and restrictions on the nature and size of marketing costs. Some consideration is also given to the regulation of the structure of commissions paid to agents, especially in the life annuity market.

The data on investment returns, which are calculated after the deduction of operating costs, show that Chilean workers did better on balance than either Malaysian or Singaporean workers, although investment returns in these two countries also benefited from the high real interest rates that prevailed in many countries during the 1980s. However, the concern in Chile arises from the realization that the very high investment returns of the 1980s are unlikely to be continued in the future and lower operating costs may then become crucial for the net financial results of the system.

Table 3   *Operating Costs and Investment Returns*

	Singapore	Malaysia	Zambia	Chile
	1990	1989	1988/9	1990
Operating Costs as per cent of				
Annual Contributions	0.53	1.99	51.7	15.4
Average Total Assets	0.10	0.18	6.8	2.3
Covered Annual Wages	0.21	0.40	5.17	1.54
Real Investment Returns on Individual Accounts (during 1980s)	2.86	4.82	-55.0*	7.5-10.5

* Guesstimate based on nominal rate of interest of 5 per cent and average inflation rate of 135 per cent.

To summarize, the Chilean scheme is a government mandated but privately managed system. It is a defined contribution system based on individual capitalization accounts. It is very simple and transparent and is supported by strict and effective regulation and supervision. The system benefits from important government guarantees that include the provision of minimum pensions, which implies that it is not strictly speaking a mono-pillar system. Over the first ten years of its existence, the Chilean system has achieved abnormally high real rates of return, but it has also been characterized by very high operating costs.

Swiss Chilanpore: The way forward?

The idea of Swiss Chilanpore is based on a pension reform strategy that combines the best features of each country, while avoiding their weaknesses. Thus, a reformed pension system would be a multi-pillar system comprising two compulsory pillars and one or two voluntary ones.

The inclusion of compulsory pillars is based on the need to support retired workers with low lifetime earnings and limited savings (redistribution) and on the presumption that individuals, especially younger workers, are myopic with respect to their retirement needs and will not save adequately for their old age (forced saving). It is also based on the need to discourage moral hazard and free riding behaviour by those who fail to provide for their old age and intend to rely on the generosity and charity of their fellow human beings. Given the way society treats the very poor and homeless people, this argument has always sounded to me a little spurious and a concoction of academic theoreticians. But although one may have doubts about its practical significance, it is difficult to deny its intellectual relevance. Compulsory participation may be a more pragmatic consideration in overcoming the adverse selection bias that afflicts annuity markets. Finally, an important factor is the provision of insurance against correlated risks such excessive longevity and high inflation.

Whatever the rationale for compulsory participation, it is important to emphasize the responsibility of government to ensure that compulsory pillars function properly, are fair and equitable, and achieve their financial and social objectives. However, government also has a responsibility to regulate and supervise voluntary pillars, especially if it provides fiscal incentives for their promotion or, as is almost always the case, the private markets suffer from information asymmetries and the problems of moral hazard, adverse selection, agency costs and free riding mentioned in the introduction of this paper. Thus, government has a role to play even in the case of voluntary pillars, although its responsibility is clearly much stronger in the case of compulsory ones.

The first pillar

The first pillar would be a defined benefit plan and would follow the approach of the Swiss first pillar. It would be based on the principles of solidarity (i.e. it would operate on a "pay-as-you-go" basis) as well as the principles of proportionality, indexation and actualization, and lifetime earnings. As in the Swiss system, the first pillar would consist of two parts: a flat-rate full-career minimum pension; and an earnings-related pension. In addition, a public assistance pension, perhaps equal to half the minimum pension and subject to strict means testing, could be paid to old people with insufficient means.

The first part would pay a minimum pension that would be fixed irrespective of salary level. The full minimum pension would be paid for a career of say 40 years (though a shorter or longer full working career may be used) and would be pro-rated by the actual length of each worker's career. The minimum pension could be set equal to 15 per cent or 20 per cent of average earnings. Ideally, all pension payments should be linked to net earnings, i.e. earnings after the deduction of payroll contributions to the pension system. This part would have a redistributive objective.

The second part of the first pillar pension would be earnings-related. It would be based on average actualized lifetime earnings and could amount to an additional 15 per cent to 20 per cent of net average earnings. Actualization of lifetime earnings could be based on the wage index or on the price index. The second part would provide an affordable level of intergenerational insurance with regard to a desirable minimum replacement rate for workers with average wages and full careers.

Both elements of the first pillar pension would be indexed, although the choice of indexation could be either to prices or to wages. Perhaps, the Swiss solution of using the arithmetic mean of the two indices would be a good compromise, especially in countries where real wages do not follow a constant upward trend.

The contribution rate for the first pillar would depend on the demographic structure of the labour force. A rate between 5 per cent and 10 per cent would be adequate for most countries. In addition, a reasonable state contribution might be appropriate. If the old age dependency ratio were to increase to such an extent as to require a higher contribution rate for financial equilibrium of the first pillar, consideration should be given to increasing the normal retirement age (or what amounts to the same thing, an increase in the length of a full career). This would clearly lower the old age dependency ratio or the effective replacement rate and would mitigate the financial pressures on the pillar.

The second pillar

The second pillar would be a defined contribution plan with individual capitalization accounts. It would be based on the principles of private management and individual choice, simplicity and transparency, safety and profitability, strict regulation and effective supervision, and operating efficiency.

The second pillar would aim to pay a pension equal to 30 per cent to 40 per cent of actualized average lifetime net earnings (or of final year net earnings). There would be a minimum rate of contribution that would be set in the light of projected growth rate of real wages, real rates of return, and normal lengths of working and retirement lives. A contribution rate between 10 per cent and 15 per cent would be adequate, unless there was a big negative gap between real returns and the growth of real earnings. Because the first pillar would be based on a combination of a flat-rate full-career minimum pension and a lifetime-earnings-related pension, individual workers could be allowed to increase their contribution rates (up to a specified ceiling) if the second pillar were to be based on final year earnings in order to achieve a 70 per cent integrated replacement rate. The fiscal treatment would be based on tax deferral to provide an incentive for compliance, although to minimize its regressive impact, tax deferral could take the form of tax credits rather than full deductibility of contributions.

The second pillar would be very similar in structure and regulation to the Chilean system, except in one very important respect. To avoid the apparently excessive level of operating costs, the system would include a central agency that would be responsible for record keeping, collecting contributions, paying pensions and sending out financial statements. The central agency could be a public body or it could be jointly owned by all the private companies that would be allowed to participate in the investment management of the pension funds. Its role would be similar to that of a clearing house in banking or futures markets.

The investment of pension funds would, however, be entrusted to authorized and well regulated and supervised private companies. Individual workers would have the choice to transfer the management of their funds between different companies, although account switching would then involve little more than a series of appropriate entries in the computer of the central operating agency. As in the case of Chile, investment rules would emphasize safety and profitability, there would be limits to ensure adequate diversification of risks, and there would be strict regulation and supervision by an appropriate supervisory agency. To keep marketing costs under control, there would be strict rules on advertising and a regulation of the structure of commissions paid to agents. There would also be detailed rules on the sale of annuity products.

Consideration could be given to limiting the range of products offered by both pension fund management companies and by life insurance companies. For instance, the regulations could include such rules as "one account per worker" and "one investment fund per fund management company", which are essential elements of the current Chilean scheme. Alternatively, pension management companies could be allowed to offer a small range of investment funds (say, an equity, bond and money market fund), but the allocation of individual account balances among these three funds could follow strict age-related rules. Similarly, limits could be imposed on the offer of annuity products, perhaps opting for life annuities with ten year certain payments.

These restrictions on the range of products under offer could be justified on the grounds that allowing unlimited individual choice in the selection of investment funds and annuity products would go against the myopic behaviour argument for justifying the institution of compulsory pillars in the first place. The risk aversion of unsophisticated investors who tend to select short-term, low-yielding instruments that are not suitable for the long-term contractual nature of these savings would be another justification.

As the second pillar would be a defined contribution plan, indexation of balances would not be appropriate. However, balances may be protected from the vagaries of high and volatile inflation by requiring or encouraging pension funds to invest in indexed long-term securities or in instruments that provide effective hedges against inflation. On the other hand, annuity products should be fully indexed.

A possible variation in this approach would be to entrust the central agency with the selection of investment fund managers on the basis of transparent procedures and clear investment guidelines. This would minimize marketing costs and would ensure that all workers participate in the same national pool. The risk of political interference with the utilization of funds and the awarding of fund management contracts would be strong arguments against such centralization of decision making, though adequate safeguards could be developed. This approach is being gradually adopted by the Employees Provident Fund of Malaysia, though its experience with the new approach, which has been prompted by the reduced borrowing needs of the Malaysian Government, is still limited.

Voluntary pillars

In addition to the compulsory pillars, voluntary pension schemes may also be set up. These could be created by employers or they could be established by individuals who would like to aim for higher replacement ratios than those envisaged under the compulsory pillars. As a rule, voluntary schemes should benefit from the same fiscal incentives as the compulsory pillars. In general, the fiscal treatment should allow the deductibility of contributions (perhaps up to specified ceilings) and exemption of investment income (perhaps also up to specified limits), while pensions should be treated as any other source of income.

Although voluntary, employer pension schemes should be regulated to protect the interests of workers and ensure equitable and non-discriminatory treatment. Thus, there should be minimum vesting and portability provisions, while in defined benefit schemes, pensions should be based on actualized average lifetime earnings rather than final year earnings (this would eliminate the favourable treatment of senior managers and other high fliers). There should also be prudential, fiduciary and custodial regulations, though given the financial responsibility of employers detailed investment rules may not be necessary.

The scope for voluntary company-based schemes would be much more limited under a system with two compulsory pillars. To the extent that companies need to encourage loyalty and firm-specific training or to operate flexible employment policies, they would have to develop alternative compensation schemes that would be unrelated to the provision of occupational pensions.

Voluntary personal pension plans and annuity products would also need to be regulated to protect the interests of consumers. Such regulation and supervision should follow broadly similar lines to that of banking and insurance companies and should emphasize stability, efficiency and fairness.

Concluding remarks

This paper has addressed some of the issues raised in establishing a pension system. The main focus has been on creating a system that can cope well with the objectives of solidarity, redistribution and insurance against correlated risks, operating and investment efficiency, and accumulation of sufficient balances for the payment of adequate but affordable pensions.

The paper does not discuss several important issues such as ensuring high coverage and compliance with the compulsory pillars of the system, the interaction between regulation and financial market development, or the problems of transition. Two points that should perhaps be stressed is that the proposed new structure envisages a continuing, though reduced, role for a public pension pillar and a much reduced role for company-based pension schemes.

A question that might be raised is why favour a Swiss Chilanpore system and not a Dutch one. The main difference between the first pillars of the Netherlands and Switzerland is that the Dutch system includes only a flat-rate pension under its first pillar. This is targeted at about 40 per cent of average earnings and is financed with contributions from all residents equal to 14.8 per cent of their earnings. The cost of the Dutch system is clearly much higher than the Swiss. Although flat-rate systems are preferred by economists because they involve fewer distortions in incentives, the existence of an earnings-related part in the first pillar would help provide some insurance about a minimum replacement rate for workers with full careers and average earnings. A less generous flat rate system than the Dutch one would fail to provide a floor to the replacement rate. Thus, the argument for including two parts in the first pillar is very much one of keeping costs down while minimizing risks by diversifying across different providers.

The much reduced role of occupational pension schemes can be justified on two grounds. First, occupational pension schemes suffer from many shortcomings related to intentional and unintentional redistribution among members of different schemes. To the extent that they are used as a personnel management tool, they are bound to penalize some workers more than others. Eliminating these shortcomings by appropriate regulations regarding minimum vesting, portability and indexation standards would weaken the incentive of employers to continue sponsoring such plans. The second argument is that, with declining stability in employment patterns, company-based schemes would become exceedingly unsuitable for providing employment-based social benefits such as pension and health insurance.

Finally, a word of caution is needed about the applicability and relevance of a pension reform strategy based on the outlines of this proposal. Despite the rhetorical question in the introduction of this paper, there is really no blueprint for any type of reform that can be applied in all countries, regardless of local circumstances and conditions. For instance, in countries where national provident funds have failed patently, as has been the case in most African countries, because of underdeveloped capital markets, weak administration, and political interference, the proposed multi-pillar structure would not have many chances of success, unless capital markets were reformed and the regulatory machinery was much strengthened and improved. In such countries, social insurance systems might be a preferable alternative at this juncture, especially if they benefit from very favourable demographic structures and if they are properly designed to avoid the distortions that have afflicted the social insurance systems of Latin American and Eastern European countries. However, governments in such countries should not lose sight of the need to reform further their emerging social insurance systems in the long run and to restructure them in due course towards the multi-pillar approach advocated in this paper.

References

Asher, Mukul. 1991. *Social Adequacy and Equity of the Social Security Arrangements in Singapore.* Centre for Advanced Studies, National University of Singapore, Occasional Paper No. 8, Singapore.

CPF. 1990. *Annual Report 1990.* Central Provident Fund Board, Singapore.

Davis, E.P. 1992. *The Structure, Regulation and Performance of Pension Funds in Nine Industrial Countries.* World Bank, CECFP, mimeo.

Gillion, Colin; Bonilla, Alejandro. 1992. "Analysis of a National Private Pension Scheme: The Case of Chile". *International Labour Review*, 131 (2). Geneva, International Labour Office.

OECD. 1988. *Switzerland, Economic Survey 1987/88.* Paris, OECD.

Queisser, Monika. 1991. "Social Security Systems in South East Asia", *International Social Security Review*, 44 (1-2). Geneva, International Social Security Association.

Schwarz, Anita M. 1992. *Basic Parameters of Mandatory Retirement Savings Schemes.* World Bank, CECFP, mimeo.

Schwarz, Anita M.; Vittas, Dimitri. 1992. *Policy Issues in Pension Guarantees.* World Bank, CECFP, mimeo.

Vittas, Dimitri. 1992. *The Simple(r) Algebra of Pension Plans.* World Bank, CECFP, mimeo.

Vittas, Dimitri; Iglesias, Augusto. 1992. *The Rationale and Performance of Personal Pension Plans in Chile.* World Bank, Working Paper Series 867.

Vittas, Dimitri; Skully, Michael. 1991. *Overview of Contractual Savings Institutions.* World Bank, Working Paper Series 605.

Wyatt. 1990. *Benefits Report — Europe, USA.* Brussels, The Wyatt Company SA.

6

Structural adjustment policies and their implications for social security in Latin America[1]

Rodolfo Saldain
President
Social Insurance Bank
(Uruguay)

Worlwide trends

During the last ten years developments in the economic and social field have been proceeding in a worldwide context dominated by a period of triumph for economic liberalism and, more recently, the collapse of the system of political and economic organization which previously prevailed in the geographical and ideological regions which had Moscow as their centre.

However, the economic system based on the private ownership of the means of production and on the market as the free regulator of the supply and demand of goods, services and factors has changed radically since the time of the Industrial Revolution. The changes which have taken place relate fundamentally to the roles reserved respectively for the state, society and the individual.

---

1. The opinions expressed here are the sole responsibility of the author and do not commit in any way the institution he represents.

The first sign of the emergence of the state as a factor in the economic and social spheres is the birth of the Welfare State. This was the beginning of a new trend, involving the strengthening of the roles of the state and society vis-à-vis the individual. The first signs of the reversal of that trend appeared at the end of the 1970s, when the roles of the individual, private enterprise and the market began to regain importance.

Trends in the region

Post-war development strategies

The prevalence of underdevelopment, the scandalous situation in which extreme poverty contrasted with extreme wealth, the growing conviction that the classical instruments of economic theory were inadequate and the need to include the element of power in the analysis as an essential factor in the interpretation of social and economic realities in the region led a substantial group of thinkers in Latin America to seek to develop their own line of thinking.

In that context the state was envisaged as a primary economic agent and the principal creator and promoter of all processes of change. The protection of import-substituting industrialization which that approach implied, on the basis of which the greater part of local industry developed, gave rise in the latter to a high degree of dependency on subsidies and high rates of customs duties. This situation, together with the absence of competition, offered little incentive for the improvement of efficiency.

Moreover, the populist orientations of many governments facilitated thedevelopment of mechanisms which gave rise to budget deficits, galloping inflation and macroeconomic imbalances generally.

The "creeping" crisis

The "oil shock" of the 1970s affected the countries of the region in a diametrically opposite fashion according to whether they were importers or exporters of oil.

It forced the great majority of the countries of the region to increase their foreign indebtedness substantially, and all of them were affected thereby in much the same way.

The principal factors which gave rise to the crisis, after several years of a steady falling-off in external demand, were the sudden fall in the net return on capital which occurred in 1982 and the great increase in net financial transfers abroad in the form of profits and interest payments which occurred at the same time (Cepal[2], 1986, p. 16).

The cumulative effect of these developments, coming as they did on top of the rundown or failure of postwar development strategies, was to give rise to a "creeping" regional crisis essentially undermining economic, social and political systems.

External imbalance

The crisis obliged debtor countries to face up to a current balance of payments deficit equal to 40 per cent of the value of exports of goods and services; under the new circumstances this could not continue to be financed through net revenue from loans or investments. Consequently, the region has been forced to begin a processs of readjustment (Cepal, 1986, p.16).

As has been noted, the region as a whole has succeeded in reducing the external imbalance with extraordinary speed. However when the manner by which it was achieved is taken into account, this marked reduction of the current account deficit has been very costly in terms of declining economic activity and employment (Cepal: 1986).

Structural adjustment programmes

Need for structural adjustment

The hoped-for effects of structural adjustment policies – such as the reduction of macroeconomic imbalances, fiscal discipline and the lowering of inflation rates – are all lacking in attributes which a government can set itself as long-term policy aims. However, there can be little doubt that these effects are prerequisites for the achievement of any long-term policy objectives – or, in more high-flown terms, of any ultimate Utopia, whatever its nature, one is seeking to attain.

It is commonly argued that the pursuit of stability must be accompanied by structural adjustments designed to eliminate factors perceived as putting a brake on economic development and as possibly giving rise to new imbalances which would render efforts to achieve stability nugatory. Since some of the

---

2. Economic Commission for Latin America and the Caribbean (United Nations)

attributes of economic development can develop into long-term objectives, the strategies adopted to promote that development are relevant from the stand-point of the results to be achieved.

Contents of structural adjustment programmes

It has become customary to speak of two types of structural adjustment proposals — orthodox and heterodox. Generally speaking, the recommenda-tions of the multilateral financing organizations, which are based on neo-liberal economic thinking, are included in the former category.

In contrast, the attempts at adjustment made by some governments in the region over the last ten years fall into the second category. Invariably these attempts have failed to lead to recovery of the investments made within a time-frame within which even polices of the kinds adopted could be considered viable and have given rise to situations in which control of economic affairs has been lost and threats to political control, and even to the structure of the entire system, have emerged (Calderon *et al.* 1990, p. 53). The periods of government of Raul Alfonsin in Argentina and Alan Garcia in Peru are usually presented as examples of experiences of this kind.

Following the failure of these heterodox experiments with structural adjust-ment, orthodox polices appeared almost inevitable.

These structural adjustment policies fall generally under one of four head-ings: trade and price policies; public investment policies; budget policies; and policies designed to promote the more efficient mobilization of resources. Within this category the World Bank is promoting reforms of a type known as institutional reforms (Lichtensztejn *et al.*, 1986, p.177).

Structural aspects of social security in Latin America

Notwithstanding considerable differences from country to country, one can observe certain common features in social security programmes in Latin Ameri-ca which recur over and over again, either as regards time-frames or in the different stages of development they are passing through. Likewise, com-parative studies have revealed certain features which are not only common to national schemes but also reflect patterns of social protection throughout the entire region.

One may consider these common and recurrent features as structural features of social security in Latin America and on that basis endeavour to present them in various ways. Particular mention should be made of the following features.

Wide-ranging differences within the region

The degree or stage of development reached in the programmes of the different countries in the region varies considerably from one to another. There is now a well established classification of countries based on the unweighted average of 11 preselected variables. This method divides the countries concerned into three groups (Mesa-Lago, 1985, p. 346):

- Advanced levels:
  Uruguay, Argentina, Chile, Cuba, Brazil, Costa Rica

- Intermediate levels:
  Panama, Mexico, Peru, Colombia, Bolivia, Ecuador, Paraguay, Venezuela

- Low levels:
  Dominican Republic, Guatemala, El Salvador, Nicaragua, Honduras, Haiti.

This differentiation touches on matters relating to production in the countries concerned. The scope for diversification of production − particularly with regard to the emphasis on production for export implicit in structural adjustment policies − is in this regard affected in two ways:

- The countries with relatively high levels of social development have greater scope for diversification of their production at internationally acceptable quality levels. At the same time, the levels of skills implicit in those levels of social development generally reflect higher labour costs and consequently imply higher prices for their export products.

- On the other hand, the low cost (including social security contributions) of labour may be considered as a comparative advantage enjoyed by the great majority of the countries in the region.

The differences existing within the region are taking on a new significance within the framework of the process of regional integration currently under way. For instance, the Treaty of Asuncion establishing the Southern Common Market (MERCOSUR), the signatories to which are Argentina, Brazil, Paraguay and Uruguay, provides for freedom of movement of goods, services and production factors among the four countries. The implication of this development is that the differences between national social security programmes in the region will have two effects, neither of them in principle desirable:

- As regards the possibility of freedom of movement of workers, the levels of social protection enjoyed by the latter will vary substantially from country to country; and in addition there is no minimum level of legislative co-ordination and no simple procedure for recognition or protection of acquired rights.

- At the same time, the differences will create distortions unfavourable to the countries with higher levels of social development, since their production will be more costly in terms of the human resources involved.

The tendency for power structures to reproduce themselves

The great majority of programmes originated in sectors with a substantial measure of power, and the gradual spread of coverage throughout the population followed similar patterns; generally speaking, the lower income groups within the population remained outside the system.

It can be said in general terms that significant sectors of the population succeeded in attaining levels of consumption similar to those prevalent in developed countries, obtained admission to decision-making circles and secured a share of economic, social and political power; but at the same time the majority of the population was excluded and received little or nothing of the benefits of progress (Sainz, 1987, p. 66).

This tendency for dominant power structures to reproduce themselves is mainly apparent in two areas — the restriction of coverage within the population; and the neutral or even negative application of the solidarity principle.

Restriction of coverage within the population

In Latin America social security programmes follow, with regard to the risks and contingencies covered, an occupation-based model of coverage.

In my analysis of the models for the coverage of the contingencies of invalidity, old age and survivors' provision (Saldain, 1991) I identified three possible types of coverage — universal; occupation-based; and selective.

As the scope of the programmes in force in the region is fundamentally occupation-based, large groups of disadvantaged persons are not covered. This type of coverage corresponds, broadly speaking, to the model developed by Bismarck.

The population groups below the poverty line in Latin America are normally not protected by social insurance (Mesa-Lago, 1989, p. 68).

This restriction of coverage within the population has given rise to another feature of a structural nature, which is also bound up with patterns of distribution of power and the integrative or exclusive nature of the dominant development strategies, namely a marked bias of coverage in favour of the towns, and even of the capital city.

The process of social integration which began in the 1950s was essentially confined to urban areas; it was based mainly on a mobilization of the social groups in those areas; and, with a few exceptions, it tended to favour them over social groups in rural areas. The establishment of the legitimacy of the social system and of patterns of control of society was linked to the expansion of economic structures, and in particular the modern and dynamic sectors of those structures; this expansion enabled certain extensions of coverage to be introduced, albeit on a selective basis. However, the scope for further incorporation of the growing mass of the urban population within the modern sector of the economy has declined, and these groups are now finding access to social security and to active participation in political and cultural life increasingly difficult (Sainz, 1987, p. 78).

In the countries of Latin America in the intermediate group, less than half the population is covered, and in those in the lowest-level group less than a quarter. The English-speaking countries in the Caribbean, thanks to a spirit of political compromise, the British model and certain geographical advantages, have succeeded in attaining almost universal coverage (Mesa-Lago, 1989, p. 154).

Neutral or negative application of the solidarity principle

This is the second component of the tendency of dominant power structures to reproduce themselves. It implies that the scheme reproduces (neutral application) or aggravates (negative application) the inequalities existing within society as a whole.

Social security programmes operate by levying resources from a "providing" population group and transferring them, in the same or some other form, to a "recipient" group. These compulsory transfers of the resources of individuals affect the community-wide distribution of incomes. In principle their effects may be neutral, or they may lessen or aggravate the income inequalities already existing in a given community.

Where the effect is neutral, the providing and recipient population groups are identical, and the programme in question certainly serves as an instrument of temporary reallocation of resources on a basis of principles of commutative justice and synallagmatic relationships, in which, at the level of the individual, the contributory input (levy) is seen as equal to the amount of benefit or services received.

Where the effect of the scheme is to reduce inequalities of income, the providing and recipient population groups are not identical, or at least the amount levied from a provider should bear a direct relationship to the income while the amount paid to a recipient should not. In this case the programme acts as an instrument of redistribution of resources among social groups on a basis of principles of distributive justice and equity.

Finally, if the effect of a social security programme is to aggravate or widen inequalities of income, the levying process will tend to enlarge the providing population group — or even, if possible, concentrate its effects on the lower-income groups — whereas the benefits will tend to be concentrated on persons with higher incomes than the providers. In this case the programme acts as an inequitable instrument of reallocation of resources among social groups, and its origins will generally have to be recognized as deriving from dominant power patterns.

Only rarely can a particular programme be classified squarely within one of the three categories just mentioned. However, there is a tendency for one principle or another to predominate. In Latin America the majority of programmes have tended to seek to expand or widen the providing population group — bringing within its scope persons with relatively low incomes — while restricting the size of the recipient group to include only groups of persons with relatively high incomes.

This situation is the result of the application of the Bismarckian model of tripartite financing in the actual conditions prevailing in Latin America. The transfers of state resources and of employer contributions (wherever it has been possible to pass them on in prices) have resulted in an expansion or widening of the providing group, i.e., the group of persons subject to levies. This is particularly serious where — as is the case in the majority of the countries in the region — tax revenue is derived from taxes on consumption. On the other hand, the limited scope of the cover provided tends to restrict the number of recipients.

According to Mesa-Lago (1989, p. 25), an insured person does not pay more than one-third of the cost of the protection he receives. This situation he considers unfair in countries where only a small proportion of the population is covered.

In this context it often happens that persons with relatively low incomes are excluded from the group of beneficiaries notwithstanding the fact that they are often included among the providers of resources. In other cases they may form part of the group of recipients but receive benefits of a standard significantly lower that that of those given to persons with relatively high incomes. This situation is based, not on principles of commutative justice, but on privilege secured through relationships with the power structure.

The hegemony of public administration

The development of social security in the region has proceeded in line with that of organizations in the public sector. Only in exceptional cases is the administration of programmes in the hands of associations or private bodies.

Public administration in Latin America suffers from serious failings. These failings are to be found in organizations responsible for the administration of social security programmes, whether they form part of the central administration of the State or operate in a decentralized fashion.

Social security administration in Latin America has been characterized by high cost, inadequacies in the training of its managers and in the technical organization of its functions, excessive bureaucracy, a lack of efficiency criteria and a predominantly romantic and voluntarist outlook on the part of its senior administrators. In addition, it has not been free of corruption of different types.

A tendency to develop financial and actuarial deficits

When launching their programmes – particularly those relating to the contingencies of old age, invalidity and provision for survivors – most of the countries of the region introduced funding-based schemes.

From full funding they moved on, in stages which are clearly identifiable in the histories of all the countries in the region which have achieved relatively advanced levels of social development, to partial funding and finally to entirely pay-as-you-go schemes.

The process of introduction of reforms within systems – particularly in the countries in the region which had achieved relatively advanced levels of social development – encountered serious difficulties of a political nature which frequently proved insurmountable obstacles. In some countries, where the need for reform was particularly pressing, the political authorities sought to avoid them for many years, thus giving rise to a number of consequences which today can clearly be seen to have been totally negative. The two principal means of sidestepping the problems and putting off their solution were, firstly, the generation of budget deficits, and secondly, the significant reduction in the levels of benefits.

During the 1980s this tendency was aggravated by the effects of the recession, unemployment and the growth of the informal sector.

The inadequacy of planning

Social security programmes in the region have been developed in an almost completely unplanned fashion, on a basis of seriously deficient technical and academic knowledge and in a context of flowery language poured forth both by politicians and by academic circles.

Proper planning permits the establishment of programmes which will achieve the desired objectives. Once an informed and clear definition of what it is desired to achieve has been established, a programme which will serve as an instrument for achieving that objective can be drawn up.

For social security as in any other field, the planning process requires a minimum basis of information. In many of the countries of the region one of the many deficiencies of the public service is the lack of an information base adequate for this purpose. Consequently the assembly of this information should be a priority task.

One result of this situation has been that, with a few exceptions, attempts to revise programmes are launched without sufficient assessment of their effects.

However, if we assume that the objectives of social security are those which can be deduced from the romantic and voluntarist pronouncements we hear, it can be affirmed that the level of correlation between the stated objectives and the means of attaining them is very low, since, as is stated in a recent Cepal publication (1992, p. 21), the principal shortcoming of social security systems in the region is their lack of fairness.

Structural adjustment policies and their impact on social security

First of all, a point of primary policy importance must be made. Although it is true to say that structural adjustment policies imply by definition the principle of subsidiarity of the state and that no specific public policies should be required to regulate the distribution of the fruits of development — since this should take place through a natural "trickle-down" effect — one must at the same time recognize the error of assuming that the structures of all the countries concerned require the same adjustments; on the contrary, the nature and depth of the adjustments required must depend on decisions taken within each country in the light of certain dominant tendencies of a general character.

It has been pointed out (Lichtensztejn *et al*, p. 209) that loans for structural adjustment purposes provided by the multilateral financing organizations and the conditions attached to those loans are irrefutable and explicit proof of a determination to influence the overall internal policies of a number of countries. But there is another and equally important factor which has to be kept in mind, namely the relationship with these organizations, and especially with the IMF and the World Bank.

These bodies also function within patterns of thinking based on economic neo-liberalism, and they tend to reproduce mechanically sets of recommendations in the formulation of which frequently little thought is given to reality. However, we should not hold them directly responsible for the fate of our countries; rather the officials of governments in the region should endeavour to overcome the limitations of the simplistic attitude which is apparent in the recommendations of these bodies. It certainly seems desirable that the latter should give more thought to levels of professional competence in some of its missions and to the knowledge of the actual situation in the country concerned.

The process of negotiations with these bodies requires that the officials of governments in the region should have sufficient knowledge and skill to arrive at agreements which remain within the limits of what is reasonable. At the same time, however, they must not lose sight of the fact that the conclusion of such agreements is practically unavoidable. This applies both to the negotiation of external debt and to the securing of new sources of finance.

Discipline in budgeting

Discipline in budgeting affects the whole of the public sector. It has a serious impact on social security, as one of the latter's characteristic features, as we have seen, is its tendency to incur financial and actuarial imbalances.

However, public finance is severely affected by other factors, such as transfers for the servicing of external debt, which still constitutes an excessive burden on the economies concerned; this, however, would not justify the loss of political interest in the subject which seems to be occurring at present.

A budget can be brought into balance by increasing income, reducing expenditure or a combination of the two. In the field of social security the volume of expenditure is generally unchangeable in the short term — and probably in the medium term as well.

In the countries at the southern end of South America, in which the principal element of social security consists of coverage of the contingencies of old age, invalidity and provision for survivors, the limitation of expenditure is extremely difficult on account of the high level of resistance to changes in legislation. The experience of some of the countries in the sub-region demonstrates that failure to pay benefits has consequences of a legal, political and financial nature.

In the legal field there have been innumerable cases in which the defendants have been sentenced, for a variety of reasons, to pay benefits in the form prescribed by law; there have even been cases in which criminal proceedings have been instituted against social security administrators.

As a result of cases of this kind and of the general lowering of levels of benefit, social security programmes and the institutions administering them have fallen into serious disrepute, and all are enmeshed in a crisis of credibility and legitimacy. In the political field this situation has had one general effect; it has everywhere been exploited by demagogues.

A second effect of a political nature was observed in Uruguay (Saldain, 1991, p. 50). There a movement developed which led to the holding of a plebiscite in November 1989. The motion was supported by over 80 per cent of the electorate — which shows the high degree of popular support obtained. It required the insertion in the Constitution of procedures for the indexing of old-age, invalidity and survivors' benefits and specifying in detail when adjustments were to made (whenever the salaries of public officials were adjusted) and the criteria for adjustment (the average wage and salary index).

In this case the attempts to withhold fraudulently benefits legally due were clearly counterproductive from the financial standpoint, since they sparked off a popular backlash which cost more than the saving supposedly achieved by the fraudulent manoeuvring. It must be kept in mind that this policy was promoted by at least one multilateral credit institution.

Within the other major component of social security in Latin America, namely health care benefits (which in a considerable number of the countries concerned form the principal element of social security), the core problem is that of the steadily rising cost of health care. The economic crisis of the 1980s and the stabilization and structural adjustment policies all made for reductions in expenditure — at least in the initial stages — and as a general rule had a significant impact on investment in social infrastructures (education, health and housing).

As is the case in much of the rest of the public sector, the selection of means was lacking in objectivity as regards both the containment and the reduction of social expenditure. The choice of the expenditure items to be tackled and the extent to which they are to be contained or reduced is essentially a political problem. It is extremely difficult to explain why defence expenditure, for example, has not been reduced more except in terms of power positions and of the role those positions have played in the recent past.

In the area of expenditure, structural adjustment policies have sought to reduce public expenditure in the social field. Their success in this regard has varied considerably according to the country concerned and the nature of the social protection programmes in each. All the evidence suggests that expenditure on social infrastructure has suffered most, while expenditure on social security was much less affected on account of the latter's rigidity.

As regards incomes, stabilization and adjustment policies have given rise to increases in taxation. This was a response to the primary concerns of the designers of fiscal policies — the speed of collection and the certainty of securing the amount of revenue sought after.

Transfer of accumulated wealth to private ownership and concentration of its ownership

The reduction of public expenditure as an element in a policy of designed to achieve budgetary equilibrium does not have to stop at the achievement of that equilibrium. It may be pressed still further in the pursuit of reductions in taxes, especially those which cannot be passed on to consumers or which, if they can be so passed on, distort the conditions of participation in the activities of the world outside.

A high level of public expenditure, even where the budget is balanced, means that the public sector is appropriating a substantial proportion of accumulated wealth in that it is removing resources from the private sector in order to redistribute them under public policies. Structural adjustment policies and their conceptual basis of economic neo-liberalism are totally hostile to the allocation of resources through the state, and instead demand that this role should be left to the market.

It is thus proposed that the public appropriation of wealth should be replaced by appropriation by the private sector — in other words, that the accumulation of wealth should be privatized.

A second feature of the new pattern of appropriation of accumulated wealth is that the ownership of the latter becomes more concentrated. According to the theories under consideration here, the need for saving and investment can be met by concentration of the appropriation of wealth in private hands. Privatization of this kind by itself does no more than exclude the public sector from the appropriation process; but it does not of itself guarantee a surplus sufficient to ensure that the need for saving and investment is met. In theory it is possible for the wealth thus appropriated by the private sector to be distributed within society as a whole in such a way as to favour the consumption function.

But leaving theoretical approximations aside, the increasing stagnation of the economies of the countries of Latin America and the Caribbean during the 1980s can be related to the sharp falling-off of net investment in a number of countries. During earlier decades the expansion of productive capacity — both for export and to meet internal demand — was based on relatively high and rising levels of both public and private investment. The picture during the 1980s was completely different. The deterioration of the terms of trade and the burden of servicing foreign debts — accompanied in nearly every case by a decline in inflows of foreign capital — reduced substantially the amount of net resources available for investment. In addition, the methods used to cover budget deficits created an unfavourable outlook, discouraged private investment, weakened the financial margin for manoeuvre of the public sector and, generally speaking, deepened the crisis still further. Today many countries are confronted with a growing obsolescence of their productive equipment and an alarming rundown of their physical infrastructures as a result of these trends (Cepal, 1990, p. 38).

Attempts are being made to remedy the shortfalls in saving and investment by a strategy of privatization and concentration of the process of accumulation of wealth.

Within such a strategy a shift from the present pay-as-you-go schemes to individual funding-based schemes managed by private commercial companies can be seen to be a particularly tempting instrument inasmuch as it permits the extremely rapid accumulation of extremely large sums in the hands of a small number of management bodies highly specialized in investment.

The feasibility of creating and promoting the development of investment entities of this kind will depend on the actual situation in each country — and in particular the ability of those entities to take on the commitments entered into by the pay-as-you-go schemes, which will depend to a considerable degree on the degree of maturity of the latter and the extent of their financial disequilibrium.

The impact of a reform of this kind could have a highly deleterious effect on budgetary discipline if no means exist of absorbing the taxation imbalance to which it will give rise. The scope for conversion to privately managed individual funding-based schemes will have to be analysed in the light of circumstances in each country.

Institutional reform

The history of social protection in Latin America consists in essence of the development of the public-sector machinery designed to provide that protection. In the new overall context the changes effected in Chile are often held up as models for other countries to emulate. The reform of social insurance in Chile has created a system completely in line with structural adjustment and economic reconversion policies.

One central element in the neo-liberal proposals for structural adjustment is the reduction of the importance of the role of the state and the promotion of its gradual withdrawal from the economic sphere; its field of action would thus be confined to some social policies and the maintenance of continuity in public policy.

In this context the question is being raised in the majority of the countries of the region of defining the role of the private sector — including the commercial sector — in the provision of social welfare services in the near future.

A wide variety of proposals have been made in this regard; they range from the replacement of the public sector by the private sector in the role of principal provider of protection to participation by the private sector, in varying degrees, in the provision of cover under all national schemes. The more extreme of these two proposals has so far only been adopted by Chile; the less extreme idea of participation has already been adopted in the industrialized countries. In Latin America, according to Tamburi (1991, p. 214) the subject of the role of the private element within a social security system is being discussed with increasing interest. In his view there is abundant scope for the extension of public-sector protection within the region — and at the same time for the promotion of the provision of complementary benefits by private bodies; initially these would go exclusively to population groups with a relatively high level of ability to pay contributions. However, he points out that to make social insurance solely a matter of individual initiative and market laws would implicitly condemn large groups of the population (especially in countries with weak or unstable economies) to poverty and a life without any protection whatsoever.

The ideological premise underlying structural adjustment policies coincides with worldwide trends in the field of social protection. It militates in favour of a state of well-being based on a maximum of subsidiarity in government action and considers that the latter should be restricted to the protection of individuals in need.

The role reserved for the state in the provision of welfare services is a minimal and subsidiary one. In principle, the ideal situation would be one in which each individual provides for his own insurance (Piñera, 1991, p. 68).

One might define the values implicit in this model as follows: a strengthening of individualism and the sense of personal responsibility and, above all, a vigorous rehabilitation of the market as the best possible place for the allocation of resources.

Break-up of political clientelism

This subject does not relate specifically to structural adjustment policies. However, the process of economic reconversion requires the abandonment of certain practices current in earlier stages.

In the field of social security there are at least four factors making for the creation of clienteles within the different programmes. These are: (a) the fact that the institutions concerned are major employers; (b) the linkage of the provision of benefits with the network of political mediation between the authorities and the user; (c) a steady increase in the granting of privileged treatment for insurance purposes to particular groups; and (d) the unreasonably favourable treatment of debts incurred by employers and the state.

The combined effect of these four factors makes for the development of clientelism — a set of practices whereby the administrations of social security programmes have aligned themselves with a particular pattern of day-to-day conduct followed by the members of political and party structures, for whom securing action (or the absence of action) from the administration was not only the securing of a right, winning a dispute or evading an obligation but also the creation of a debt towards the political agent who had intervened on behalf of his "client" and subsequently expected a tangible demonstration of gratitude from him in the form of political support at the appropriate time.

In addition, as frequently the securing of a clientele functionally entails various degrees of corruption and poor standards of service for persons who are not "clients", the break-up of clientelism implies higher standards of conduct and the improvement of standards of service for all users.

The negative effects of the practice of clientelism in relation to the process of economic reconversion lies in the following factors; (a) the excessive financial cost of the bureaucracy; (b) the increase in expenditure caused by the award of benefits of doubtful legitimacy and the process known as "the amassing of privileges" (Mesa-Lago, 1977, p. 49); and (c) the distortions of free competition to which the different kinds of evasion give rise.

A few additional remarks on the last-mentioned factor seem desirable here. In the circumstances obtaining in the region, the transfer of the locomotive role to the market will imply changes in certain patterns of conduct which have developed in the relations between the state and employers. All forms of evasion constitute unfair competition; and the tolerance, to a greater or lesser degree, shown by the public authorities — traditional in the region — will seriously hamper the process of structural adjustment and economic reconversion. In the new context clientelism of this kind will also have to disappear.

It hampers the process because it is incompatible with the transparency which must be present in competition in the market, especially at a time when foreign investment is being encouraged. In the new context tax evasion runs directly counter to the overall policy currently being implemented.

Outlook for the year 2000; the future only seven years away

A new cycle of history

In contrast to the 1980s, which Cepal has designated "the lost decade", in its report for 1991 the Inter-American Development Bank (IADB) coined the phrase "the decade of hope" to designate the 1990s. Latin America will face major development challenges during the coming years. These challenges (IADB, 1991, p. 9) fall into three categories:

- the achievement of an adequate and sustained overall growth rate;

- the reduction of the incidence of absolute poverty and of income inequalities generally; and

- the conservation of natural resources and the improvement of the quality of the environment.

The report identifies four strategy orientations, namely — (a) orientation towards the outside world and integration of the hemisphere; (b) modernization through the development of the private sector; (c) the reform of the public sector; and (d) human resources development.

The report includes reforms of labour legislation within the ambit of the second of these orientations (modernization through the development of the private sector).

The IADB report for 1991 states that the reforms of labour legislation should be paralleled by reforms of the social security system and that arrangements should be envisaged for retraining and the payment of temporary unemployment benefit to workers between jobs. The report also comments on the desirability of encouraging the privatization of retirement pension schemes and of offering workers the possibility of choice between competing pension funds (IADB, 1991, p. 15).

The proposal to privatize retirement pension schemes is given added force by the third strategy orientation — the reform of the public sector. The report states that a general consensus emerged in Latin America during the 1980s to the effect that the public service should be cut back, a process of privatization launched and the process of abolishing regulations and bureaucratic shackles on the economy accelerated. However, the dismantling of the old machinery of government which has been effected in a number of countries of Latin America should not necessarily lead to a weakening of the state (IADB, 1991, p. 15).

On the other hand, the growing population pressure on public health and education services is giving rise to serious tensions within the system which in certain cases have reached critical levels. The process of orientation towards the outside world and of modernization of the economy will encounter serious bottlenecks in the area of human resources. Consequently high priority will has to be given during the 1990s to the improvement of education and health. (IADB, 1991, p. 17.)

Health and nutritional deficiencies are found precisely among the population groups which are deprived of access to other basic social services such as adequate housing, supplies of drinking water, education and employment in the formal sector (and as a consequence social security). The agenda for the 1990s should include programmes designed to alleviate poverty; but the long-term solution to the problem of poverty lies in the improvement of levels of occupational skill; this will enable more individuals to participate in the economic development process and secure a share of the fruits of progress (IADB, 1991, p. 19).

The role of the machinery of social protection

In the strategy orientations for the 1990s outlined in the IADB report for 1991, the machinery of social protection is assigned two kinds of roles.

Economic-functional role

The first of these roles is bound up with the process of economic reconversion, by means of which an adequate and sustained rate of overall economic growth may be achieved.

In this area two types of measures should be taken: (a) the introduction of temporary unemployment benefits and schemes for the retraining of workers, and, in the few countries where these exist, the amendment of the schemes where necessary; and (b) the privatization of retirement pension schemes (IADB, 1991, p. 19).

Depending on the speed at which the adjustment takes place and the way it is managed, this reshaping of the structure of production may lead to higher rates of unemployment, which will reach a maximum unless there is full mobility of capital. Thus, given the necessity of transferring human resources (including enterprises) into sectors producing tradeable goods, the countries of the region will have to develop energetic retraining and skill improvement programmes for sectors of production in which the levels of dominance of technology or of technical skills may not yet be adequate (Fallas, 1990).

Likewise, the privatization of retirement pension schemes, in addition to contributing to the objective of conferring a leading role on private enterprise during the coming era, implies the accumulation of large amounts of workers' savings under private management, with a corresponding impact on investment.

Social-integrating role

In their second role measures of social protection contribute in the short term to the reduction of absolute poverty and income disparities generally and in the medium term also to economic reconversion through human resources development.

This role calls for programmes specifically designed to alleviate situations of absolute poverty and to strengthen government action in the fields of health and education.

Specifically redistributive policies should have as a basis programmes which will, first, guarantee a minimum money income, which is essential to meet the needs of individuals which require a financial outlay (such as food, clothing and transport), and secondly, provide an adequate volume of goods and services in such vital areas as health, nutrition, education and housing. Policies in the second group are reflected in concrete terms in the social expenditure incurred by the state itself, while those in the first group are implemented through policies designed to create jobs and improve the productive capacity of the excluded groups.

There is considerable scope in the countries in the region for improvement in the allocation of government social expenditure. At present that expenditure benefits mainly population groups within which the "return on the investment" in social terms is much less than if it were directed to more needy groups. Consequently an evaluation of social expenditure in the different fields (health, education, social security, etc.) is urgently needed with a view to redirecting it into channels where it will give a higher return in terms of social betterment.

In particular there is an urgent need to strengthen social programmes in the fields of basic education, health and nutrition as means of improving the productivity of the rural labour force and thereby enabling the latter progressively to secure a minimum level of subsistence (Fallas, 1990).

Social security and the roles of social protection in the context of structural adjustment

The fields of activity of social security, considered as forming an integral part of social protection schemes, offer little in the way of contribution to the fulfilment of the two roles assigned to the latter within the process of structural adjustment. This is one of the principal reasons why a passionate discussion on the future of social security programmes is currently going on in the region.

Economic-functional role

To begin with, It must be admitted that unemployment protection programmes constitute one of the weakest aspects of social security in Latin America and the Caribbean. In only 6 of the 24 countries concerned does any protection against this contingency exist.

Pension schemes, in addition to having as their central objective the coverage of the contingencies of old age, invalidity and survivors' provision, are seen, in the light of the success of the Chilean experiment, as an economic and financial function in line with their role as an instrument for the mobilization of domestic savings and the financing of investment (Cepal, 1992, p. 165).

It is considered in some circles that the potential role of pension schemes as a stimulus to saving and investment is their only significant contribution to structural adjustment and that their central objective − the coverage of the contingencies of old age, invalidity and survivors' provision − thus becomes practically marginal. I consider this view a mistaken one.

However, coverage of these contingencies should at the very least not impinge unfavourably on the budgets for any possible type of economic development − and particularly those concerned with achieving macroeconomic equilibrium. To this end the structural tendency to allow financial and actuarial imbalances to develop in the social security schemes in the region must be overcome.

In addition, public administrations, which today are typically hegemonic, will probably have to leave more scope for operation to the private sector − not so much in the pursuit of an objective of transferring the function of accumulation of wealth into private hands as in response to the adjustments which the ending of the tendency of power structures to reproduce themselves − and the two manifestations of that tendency, namely the restriction of coverage to a limited segment of the population and the neutral or negative application of the solidarity principle − imply.

In practice, in the coverage provided by the state priority attention should be given, first, to the population groups which are practically or entirely excluded from the benefits of economic growth, and secondly to the fixing of boundaries for the action of state schemes beyond which action should be left to non-public entities.

The social-integrating role

This function of the machinery of social protection is directly linked to the will to redistribute incomes. As was stated earlier, it seeks to eliminate or reduce the incidence of extreme poverty and in addition seeks to influence income inequalities generally.

There is a measure of consensus that in most social policies there is scope for redirecting expenditure, even in a context of financial retrenchment, in such a way that its impact is concentrated on the sectors in which needs are greatest.

In the area of social security, however, the scope for redistribution is less (Cepal, 1986, p. 57).

However, in the famous Beveridge Report — the original report which inspired modern social security policies — the principal concern was with poverty. Beveridge himself saw the struggle against poverty as the principal objective of social security.

Attention must therefore be particularly drawn to the existing consensus on the difficulties which social security programmes in the region would have in integrating themselves into a system of social protection the principal objective of which would be the struggle against poverty — even though this was in essence the original aim of social security policies.

This concept lies at the root of all the so-called principles of social security, which are repeated over and over again in all treatises on social security — although they are rarely set in their actual context, at least in Latin America.

In a region in which poverty is reaching alarming levels, and apart from a few programmes directed to the poorest sectors of the population, the alleviation of poverty has not been a priority objective of social security. The social security model developed in the region may well have been adequate for other times and to achieve other aims; but today it is no longer adequate. For the excluded majorities it plays neither an economic-functional role nor one of social integration. It is not economically functional nor does it play a social integrationist role for the excluded majorities.

The social and economic context in Latin America

When deciding on the structure of a national social security system, with its central and complementary models, one must consider the context in which it will be operating, the definition of its objectives and the ensuing choice of instruments.

This process must naturally be conducted within each country. However, we can identify certain features of the social and economic situation in the region which may help us to lay down some general lines of orientation for the structural adjustment of social security.

Economic growth

During the last 10 years trends in gross domestic product per head at constant market prices in Latin America and the Caribbean have been markedly unfavourable to the development of social security. The average annual growth rate was negative in 1981 and 1982, slightly positive during the years 1983-87 and again negative during the closing years of the decade. The only consistent exception was Chile, but in spite of this situation of that country one must always keep in mind what emerges from the following analysis of the situation of poor households in that country.

The spread of poverty

The information available on the scale of poverty in Latin America is highly disquieting.

The information supplied by Cepal distinguishes between households in a state of poverty and those in a state of indigence. Households in the first category are defined as those with incomes of less than twice the cost of a basket of basic foodstuffs; this group includes those in the second category, which consists of households with incomes of less than the cost of a basket of basic foodstuffs.

From the information available the following table, which shows the percentage of households in each of the countries concerned in a state of poverty, has been constructed.

The case of Chile is of particular interest for purposes of this analysis. If one compares the figures for 1970 and 1990 (Cepal, 1992, p. 45) it will be seen that the numbers of households in a state of poverty or indigence has increased dramatically, even running against the very slight trend observed in the region as a whole.

The proportion of all households in a state of poverty in 1990 was double that for 1970, having risen during that period from 17 per cent to 35 per cent. Moreover, the percentages in rural and urban areas were practically identical in 1990, which meant that the percentage in the latter had trebled — from 12 per cent in 1970 to 34 per cent in 1990. A similar pattern was observed in the percentage of households in a state of indigence, which rose from 6 to 12 per cent.

It can thus be said that economic growth does not necessarily bring with it an alleviation of situations of poverty and indigence but that, on the contrary, there may well be cases in which economic growth is accompanied by an increase in the numbers of such situations.

If the objective were to be set of reducing the numbers of households in a state of poverty or indigence one could not rely exclusively on the "trickle down" effect of growth; it would be necessary to implement policies specifically directed towards that end.

Table 1   *The scale of poverty*

Country	A	A1	A2	B	B1	B2
Guatemala	68	54	75	43	28	53
Peru	52	45	64	25	16	39
Brazil	40	34	60	18	13	34
Colombia	38	36	42	17	15	22
Chile	35	34	36	12	11	15
Panama	34	30	43	16	13	22
Mexico	30	23	43	10	6	19
Venezuela	27	25	34	9	8	14
Costa Rica	25	21	28	8	11	15
Uruguay	15	10	23	3	2	8
Argentina	13	12	17	4	3	6
Latin America	37	30	53	17	11	30

where —
A = percentage of all households in a state of poverty
A1 = percentage of urban households in a state of poverty
A2 = percentage of rural households in a state of poverty
B = percentage of all households in a state of indigence
B1 = percentage of urban households in a state of indigence
B2 = percentage of rural households in a state of indigence

N.B. Cepal does not record separate data for the other countries.

Source: Cepal, 1992a, p. 45.

Distribution of the economically active population by sector

Within the total economically active population of the countries of Latin America and the Caribbean, 32.1 per cent is engaged in agriculture, 25.7 per cent in industry and 42.4 per cent in the services sector (Cepal, 1992a, p. 42).

Table 2 shows the percentage of the economically active population engaged in agriculture in individual countries.

In all the countries in the "advanced levels" group as regards the development of social security, the percentage of the economically active population engaged in agriculture is lower than the average for the region. In contrast, in all the countries in the "low levels" group the proportion is over 10 percentage points higher than that average.

Table 2 *Percentage of economically active population engaged in agriculture, 1980*

Country	Percentage	Country	Percentage
Haiti	70.0	Mexico	36.6
Honduras	60.5	Colombia	34.2
Guatemala	56.9	Panama	31.8
Paraguay	48.6	Brazil	31.2
Nicaragua	46.5	Costa Rica	30.8
Dominican Republic	45.7	Cuba	23.8
Bolivia	45.5	Uruguay	18.8
El Salvador	43.2	Chile	16.5
Peru	40.0	Venezuela	16.1
Ecuador	38.6	Argentina	13.0
AVERAGE			32.1

Source: Cepal, 1992a, p. 42.

One might thus conclude that there is a strong inverse relationship between the level of development of social security and the proportion of the economically active population engaged in agriculture.

This conclusion would appear to indicate that the geographical distribution of the economically active population has a considerable effect on the possibilities of developing social security schemes within the region. This can be attributed to a number of factors, and in particular — (a) the traditional and antiquated system of farming which predominates in Latin America; (b) the high levels of informal activity within that sector; and (c) the tendency within the majority of social security programmes in the region to be orientated towards the urban population — and even towards that of the capital city only.

Demographic aspects

In the region as a whole, the average birth rate is high; but within this general indicator too there are marked differences between countries (Cepal, 1992a, p.13). There are three countries — Argentina, Cuba and Uruguay with low birth rates (less than 20 per 1,000). In Bolivia, Ecuador, El Salvador, Guatemala, Haiti, Honduras, Nicaragua and Paraguay, however, the birth rate is over 30 per 1,000. In addition, all the countries in the latter group belong to the group of countries with the highest percentages of their economically active populations engaged in agriculture.

Table 3, which gives figures on expectancy of life at birth, also clearly shows the extent of the differences between countries.

The age structure of the population also shows marked differences from country to country, as can be seen from Table 4.

Proportion of wage earners in economically active population

Although information on the subject is extremely difficult to obtain, it is nevertheless essential, when studying matters relating to social security programmes in the region, to make some reference, however brief, to one extremely important factor, namely the proportion of wage earners in the labour force.

Table 3 *Classification of Latin American countries by expectancy of life at birth*

Less than 65 years	65-70 years	70-75 years	Over 75 years
Bolivia	Brazil	Argentina	Costa Rica
Guatemala	Colombia	Chile	Cuba
Haiti	Ecuador	Mexico	
Peru	El Salvador	Panama	
	Honduras	Uruguay	
	Nicaragua	Venezuela	
	Paraguay		
	Dominican Rep.		

Source: Cepal, 1992a, p.15.

Table 4 *Age structure of population and dependency rates in individual countries*

Country	(1)	(2)	(3)	(4)	(5)	(6)
Argentina	30	61	9	64	49	15
Bolivia	41	55	4	82	74	7
Brazil	35	60	5	67	58	8
Colombia	36	60	4	67	60	7
Costa Rica	36	59	5	69	61	8
Cuba	23	68	9	47	34	13
Chile	31	63	6	59	49	10
Dominican Republic	38	59	3	69	64	5
Ecuador	39	57	4	75	68	7

Country	(1)	(2)	(3)	(4)	(5)	(6)
El Salvador	43	53	4	89	81	8
Guatemala	45	52	3	92	87	6
Haiti	40	56	4	79	71	7
Honduras	44	53	3	89	83	6
Mexico	38	58	4	72	66	7
Nicaragua	48	49	3	104	98	6
Panama	35	60	5	67	58	8
Paraguay	40	56	4	79	71	7
Peru	37	59	4	69	63	7
Uruguay	26	62	12	61	42	19
Venezuela	38	58	4	72	66	7
AVERAGE	36	59	5	69	61	8

Source: compilation by author from Cepal data (Cepal, 1992a, p.168).

(1) Percentage of population aged 14 or less.
(2) Percentage of population aged 15-64.
(3) Percentage of population aged 65 or over.
(4) Age groups 0-14 and 65 or over as percentage of age group 15-64.
(5) Age group 0-14 as percentage of age group 15-64.
(6) Age group 65 or over as percentage of age group 15-64.

Table 5 is concerned with the percentage of the economically active population in a relationship of subordination to an employer and receiving thereunder a remuneration known as a wage (or salary). Self-employed persons and unpaid family workers are not included. The figures thus show the wage-earning labour force as a percentage of the total.

In the view of the author there are serious limitations on the scope for extension of the application of the predominantly Bismarckian model of coverage in social security programmes in the region on account of the low proportion of wage earners — in other words, the high levels of informal activity in many of the countries of the region.

Table 5   *Proportion of wage earners in economically active population*

Country	Percentage	Country	Percentage
Cuba	94.1	Nicaragua	61.4
Uruguay	89.6	Bolivia	57.2
Chile	76.9	Dominican Republic	57.1
Venezuela	76.0	Mexico	56.8
Costa Rica	72.5	Ecuador	51.5
Argentina	71.5	Peru	50.3
Panama	69.9	Guatemala	48.9
Colombia	64.5	Honduras	46.2
Brazil	64.2	Paraguay	41.0
El Salvador	62.5	Haiti	19.2

Source: Compilation by author from Cepal data (Cepal, 1992a, p.721).

Conclusions

The wide range of different situations prevailing in the countries of the region makes it difficult to draw conclusions valid for all cases. However, by recourse to a measure of abstraction one can formulate a number of general remarks which in the author's view are applicable to a significant number of national situations. They can be briefly set forth as follows:

Structural adjustment policies are necessary

Very few people today deny the need for structural adjustments in the economies of the countries of the region. However, there is less agreement on the content of those adjustments or on the relative emphasis to be laid on the different elements of the approach to be adopted, especially in the orthodox approach.

Even so, the prevailing view in both political and technical circles is that it is necessary, among other things — (i) to achieve and maintain macroeconomic equilibrium; (ii) to orientate production towards external markets; (iii) to stimulate private initiative; and (iv) to modernize the machinery of the state.

Structural adjustment policies must embrace social security policies

The tendency to allow financial and actuarial imbalances to develop within social security programmes is incompatible with the objective of eliminating budget deficits and achieving price stability.

To deal with this malfunction in programmes action will be necessary on both the income and the expenditure sides of social security schemes with the aim of arriving at financial viability.

The first step to be taken — which will affect both income and expenditure — is the elimination of clientelism: measures to end the tolerance — legal or *de facto* — shown to certain employers with regard to payment of contributions and the privileges — again, legal or *de facto* — extended to certain categories of beneficiaries. This will as a general rule require changes in management styles and in certain practices relating to the securing of political support for electoral purposes.

Another necessary factor will be the political determination needed to stand up to the wide range of pressure groups demanding special treatment, either as regards contributions or regarding the granting of new benefits without regard for the adequacy of financing.

The implementation of structural adjustment policies may bring with it risks of a social character

The initial tendency of many officials entrusted with the implementation of structural adjustment policies is to make indiscriminate cutbacks in the field of social policy. In view of the high levels of poverty and indigence in the region, such an approach may have a highly negative social impact.

However, unquestionably the best possible use must be made of the resources available. Efficiency in the use of those resources can be achieved by directing them towards the population groups within which one unit of value will give the greatest measure of satisfaction of needs.

A strategy of this kind will require prior planning within which a clear distinction is drawn between distributive and commutative objectives and the types of instrument suitable for the attainment of each. In all cases indiscriminate cutbacks in public social expenditure must be avoided.

The structural problems of social security in the region are only partly covered by structural adjustment policies

The only specifically stated objective of these programmes are —

* to deal with the financial and actuarial imbalances existing within the programmes;
* to break the hegemony of the public administration within the programmes.

The second point is relevant, not only as a dogmatic definition, but also in as much as it will enable the efforts of the public sector to be directed towards the neediest sectors of society and open up new areas of opportunity for private agencies to offer coverage to the more privileged groups. In this way the tendency for dominant power structures to reproduce themselves can be checked and programmes can be made more socially equitable. The greater the appropriation of benefits by the groups with the most economic, political and trade union power under existing programmes, the greater the effect of such a change may be.

The opening up of this field to private benefit agencies may allow a strengthening of the activities of public agencies in the areas where poverty — in terms of power as well as of financial resources — is greatest.

The strategic reorientations currently being introduced demand a more determined approach to the other structural problems of social security in the region

Social security in the countries of Latin America has serious structural limitations which frequently render its functioning incompatible with the strategy orientations prevailing in the region.

For example, the process of integration taking place within the hemisphere demands minimum levels of co-ordination between national systems and the tackling of the wide disparities existing between them.

Equally, the necessary development of human resources in the region calls for a precise definition of objectives and of the instruments chosen to attain them. It will also be necessary to give priority to the coverage of certain risks or contingencies. This implies the remedying of the inadequate planning which was a feature of the launching and development of the majority of our social security programmes. Another factor giving rise to pressures for action of this kind is the necessary reconversion of the productive machinery of the countries of the region.

Dealing with situations of poverty and indigence is a moral imperative

Poverty and indigence constitute one of the most serious and urgent of all the problems of Latin America. Social security cannot ignore them. The elimination of poverty and indigence is a fundamental aim of modern social security — even though that may have revolutionary implications in the current Latin American context. The achievement of this aim requires measures to check the tendency of power structures to reproduce themselves and to remedy the deficiencies in the planning of programmes.

It may be concluded from the foregoing that structural adjustment policies, if applied with caution, can offer significant assistance to social security, but that by themselves they constitute only a partial approach to the need to reformulate social protection programmes, since they only relate to the economic-functional aspects of those programmes. The social-integrating role of social security programmes demands more in-depth analysis than that implied by structural adjustment policies, effected within an adequate planning framework. Social security needs more than a reform; it needs a radical **rebuilding** on bases and principles different from those which have governed the launching and development so far of social security in the region.

Bibliography

Banco Interamericano de Desarrollo 1991. *Informe 1991*. Progreso Economico y Social en América Latina.

Calderon, Fernando y Dos Santos, Mario. 1990. Hacia un Nuevo Orden Estatal en América Latina. Veinte tesis sociopolíticas y un corolario de cierre. *Nueva Sociedad No.110*. Caracas.

Cepal. 1986. *Crisis Económica y Políticas de Ajuste, Estabilización y Crecimiento*. Cuadernos de la Cepal. No. 54. Santiago de Chile.

—. 1990. *Transformacion Productiva con Equidad*. La tarea prioritaria del desarrollo en América Latina y el Caribe en los años noventa. Santiago.

—. 1991. *Anuario estadistico de América Latina y el Caribe*. Edición 1990. Santiago.

—. 1992. *Equidad y Transformación Productiva: Un enfoque Integrado*. Santiago.

—. 1992a. *Anuario Estadistico de América Latina y el Caribe*. Edición 1991. Santiago.

Fallas, Helio. 1990. *Ajuste Estructural con Equidad Social en Centroamérica*. Mimeo.

Lichtensztejn, Samuel y Baer, Mónica. 1986 *Fondo Monetario International y Banco Mundial. Estrategisa y Politicas del Poder Financiero*. Ed. Nueva Sociedad. CET, San José de Costa Rica.

Mesa-Lago, Carmelo. 1977. *Modelos de segguridad social en América Latina*. Ed. SIAP, Buenos Aires.

—. 1985. El desarrollo de la seguridad social en América Latina. *Estudios e Informe de la CEPAL*, No. 43. Santiago de Chile.

—. 1989. *Aspectos Económico. Financieros de la Seguridad Social en América Latina y el Caribe: Tendencias, Problemas y Alternativas para el Año 2.000*. Banco Mundial. Mimeo.

Piñera, Jose. 1991. *El Cascabel al Gato. La batalla por la reforma previsional*. Ed. Zig-Zag. Santiago, 1991.

Sainz, Pedro. 1987. Crisis y Desarrollo: Presente y Futuro de América Latina y el Caribe. *Politicas de Ajuste y Grupos Más Vulnerables en América Latina* (Comp. Eduardo S. Bustelo). UNICEF. FCU. Bogotá.

Saldain, Rodolfo. 1991. Seguridad Social en el Uruguai. Un análisis en proycción y base de cambio. *Congreso Interamericano Juridico de la Seguridad Social*. Memorisa. ISSSTE, México.

—. 1991a. Modelos Alternativos para la Cobertura de los Riesgos de Invalidez, Vejez y Sobrevivencia. *La Financiación de las Pensiones en América Latina*. AISS. Buenos Aires.

Tamburi, Giovanni. 1991. La privatización de la seguridad social con referencis a la situación de América Latina. Enfoques y realidades. *II Congreso Interamericano Juridico de la Seguridad Social*. Memoria. ISSSTE. México.

7

Implications for social security of structural adjustment policies: The point of view in French-speaking Africa

Pierre Désiré Engo
Director-General
National Social Insurance Fund
(Cameroon)

Since 1985, the drop in dollar prices of Cameroon's main export products, in particular oil, cocoa, coffee, etc., and the fall in the exchange value of the dollar, have shown up major weaknesses in the economy of Cameroon, plunging it into a severe recession.

The drop in export receipts and the flight of capital resulting from the fact that local interest rates have not been competitive with those outside the country have led to a sharp reduction in the net foreign assets, causing a contraction in the liquid funds available to the national banking system, which in turn has been a serious threat to the level of activity in the country.

This situation has been reflected in Cameroon's social security system in the form of a sharp fall in receipts and a steep rise in expenditures. Several undertakings have closed down and others have reduced their personnel, with a consequent drop in the total payroll, which is the basis on which the social contributions are assessed. Those few employers who have stood up to the crisis have faced financial difficulties in paying their social security contributions. First and foremost among these employers are the state and public and semi-public bodies. At the banks, our statutory reserves, which should enable us to meet our social obligations during a time of crisis, have been consumed as a result of the reduction in the liquid assets of the Cameroon banking system.

It would appear that the aim of the structural adjustment, which is proposed as a way of overcoming the economic crisis, is to reorganize all the sectors of the economy by means of a series of measures designed to improve its overall competitiveness.

But unfortunately, while this is being carried through, large numbers of the population are continuing to suffer from the effects of the economic crisis. Their standard of living is being severely affected by the measures being taken as part of the structural adjustment. Faced with this situation, those responsible for social security are naturally concerned. In this they are not alone. There have in fact been various voices raised in sharp condemnation of the structural adjustment policy followed at the behest of the World Bank and the International Monetary Fund.

Thus, Mr. Mahbubul Haq, Adviser from the United Nations Development Programme (UNDP) states categorically that the structural adjustment policy runs counter to the interests of Africa. Furthermore during a recent international symposium held in Bordeaux (France) on *The constraints of structural adjustment in developing countries*, Mr. Jean-Louis Roy, Secretary General of the Cultural and Technical Cooperation Agency (ACCT), called into question the principle of such adjustment in the French-speaking countries. He said that whilst it is true that structural adjustment provides a model designed to promote economic equilibrium with regard to the budgetary deficit, balance of payments deficit, realistic prices, etc., the model is unsuitable for countries which are too small to allow an integrated pattern of trade. Such trade is almost non-existent at the regional and continental levels, mainly because of the uncertain nature of production and the rules governing international commerce, which hamper the free trade of many products.

What, then, is the basis for the concern of the social security administrators? In Africa in general and in Cameroon in particular, less than 20 per cent of the active population consisted of wage-earners enjoying social protection. At a time when those managing social security were planning to extend the system of social protection to the entire population, it is sad to observe that the immediate effects of the structural adjustment struck directly at the socially insured persons, a sizeable proportion of them losing even their right to such protection as a result of the loss of their job. As for those who were not socially insured, they have sunk deeper into poverty and misery. This situation creates the impression that the World Bank and the IMF are to some extent failing to comprehend the legitimate concerns of the various countries, especially in social matters, as those organizations have long neglected the social effects of the measures that they impose on our governments.

Indeed, one has to note that the reforms undertaken in Cameroon in the public, semi-public and banking sectors were aimed essentially at reducing the numbers of those employed and the total payroll costs, freezing the financial effects of promotions and reducing all types of bonuses and benefits. The immediate consequence of these measures was that almost 30,000 persons lost their jobs. So far the compensation measures have not enabled us to aid the involuntary victims of the structural adjustment to resume their active life in a satisfactory manner, as the range of provisions of a social nature included in the programme has proved quite inadequate to fulfil the "firefighting" role that it was supposed to play.

Given the high proportion of current government expenditure which the total payroll represents, it seems that the freezing of wages and salaries in our countries has been applied without any prior study of the system of pay and promotion in the public services. The wage freeze has discouraged and demotivated employees, reduced productivity, and increased corruption and fraud, with individuals using all the means available to them to make up for their loss of earnings.

Generally speaking, the only effect of the reduction in social expenditures has been to make it impossible to meet the essential needs of the population; no longer are all children able to go to school, and no longer does everybody have access to medical care or the right to decent housing.

In sum, the structural adjustment measures have had dramatic social consequences. The worsening of living conditions has led the disadvantaged social groups to revolt. More or less everywhere, economic demands are becoming linked with political ones.

Turning to the case of the National Social Insurance Fund of Cameroon, the World Bank and the IMF took the view that it should be reorganized in order to achieve financial equilibrium and make a profit. But before the structural adjustment programme initiated by these two organizations, the Fund regularly showed a large surplus. It had also become a major source of financing for government-instituted projects. Today, not only has structural adjustment brought the Fund into deficit, but in addition it can no longer even recover the substantial investments that it made in the economy. In another field, that of pensions, the World Bank and IMF experts failed to appreciate that the Fund does not operate on the basis of capitalization, but on the basis of a system of redistribution. The contributions of an insured person are not capitalized in individual accounts to pay for the benefits that he or she will receive. Furthermore, as a social security institution, the Fund aims to achieve a socially valuable result from its activities and not to make profits. It performs the useful role of encouraging and ensuring social peace. So little attention appears to have been paid to these aspects that a situation of conflict has developed between the World Bank and the Cameroon National Social Insurance Fund.

In this context I will simply refer to four examples.

● The World Bank recommends that health and social services should be brought within the responsibility of the National Social Insurance Fund. The law provided that, as a first step, health and social services should be financed by drawing on the contributions to the family allowances branch, prior to the possible later introduction of a sickness insurance scheme which could provide benefits both in cash and in kind. It is clear that to bring this function in as a subsidiary activity of the Fund would lead to the privatization of health and social services, which would in turn lead to the exclusion of a good part of the population from the provision of health care.

● The World Bank proposes that family allowances should be determined in advance and deducted from contributions by the employers themselves. This conflicts with the basic principles of social security, under which employees should have a right to benefits which is totally independent of the relationship with their employer.

● The World Bank proposes to suspend the reimbursement of medical expenses incurred during pregnancy, although this assistance reflects only the application of minimum standards of social security.

● The World Bank also suggests abolition of the right to family benefits in respect of children born outside the official marriage of the claimant: this ignores both the remarkable increase in the number of single-parent families in all societies and also the actual situation in Cameroon.

In conclusion, we reiterate our satisfaction with the excellent initiative taken by the ISSA in organizing this Symposium. We thank the participating international organizations for the opportunity to have a free exchange of opinions on social insurance questions. In our view this is only a beginning of the debate on this subject and we consider that it should be further developed.

We would like the World Bank, the International Monetary Fund, the International Labour Office, the ISSA and the World Health Organization to set up combined teams to examine how to assist our countries. In this context it seems to us quite essential for those responsible for social security in each country to participate in defining the new approaches needed for the economies and the institutions of Third World countries so that it is possible to continue to promote real, dynamic and self-sustaining economic growth.

8

Implications for social security of structural adjustment policies in English-speaking Africa

Henry G. Dei
Director-General
Social Security and National Insurance Trust
(Ghana)

*I*n tackling such a topic it is essential that we examine the various aspects of structural adjustment programmes — the reasons for their consideration in the first place, their preparation and their implementation. The first part of my commentary covers these three aspects. The second part examines the impact of structural adjustment and proposes an acceptable framework and role for social security under these circumstances.

Reasons for structural adjustment programmes

Fundamentally, the need for structural adjustment programmes can be attributed to the attempt by new nation states to make a quantum jump from their peasant and subsistence agricultural — based economies to modern industrialized nations overnight by following inappropriate economic blueprints based more on emotions and dreams than reality.

In addition to these inappropriate economic policies we must recognize the following factors:

- the many internal weaknesses arising from political distortions and inefficient management;

- the immense complexity of the cultural and social dimensions of the process of development;

- the resistance to changes in the status quo by the intellectual elite who were expected to spearhead the process of development; and

- the emergence of communist ideology versus the capitalist system which created a great divide.

These, among several other factors, resulted in the failure of several economic development programmes, thereby leading the way for the introduction of structural adjustment programmes.

Preparation of structural adjustment programmes

The term structural adjustment connotes total redirection of the very structure of the state and the economy. In preparing such a programme one must accept that the economy is in a state of crisis and, therefore, poses dangers as well as opportunities for redirection.

These opportunities should be viewed in terms of long term sustainability of the economy and against the ad-hoc and short term programmes provided by most structural adjustment programmes. The conventional approach has been to concentrate on the key economic indicators and provide short-term solutions aimed at correcting any imbalances, but this approach often tends to ignore the human factor and hence the programmes are invariably derailed.

The IMF and World Bank have adopted two distinct approaches:

- In the earlier periods of structural adjustment, certain programmes worked out by the IMF were imposed on the countries seeking assistance; these programmes were within the framework of prescribed agreements with bilateral and multilateral donors, following round table discussions under the auspices of the Fund.

- In the latter years, following the realization of the importance of the human factor, the IMF approach has been that the programmes proposed should emanate from the countries seeking assistance.

It must be noted that we are not attempting to apportion blame but we are dealing with improvements in a relatively young discipline which is subject to several unknown variables.

Implementation of structural adjustment programmes

Invariably, in the past, once the structural adjustment programme had been agreed to, all the measures were implemented without delay. It has been found that as a result of such hasty implementation the population is subjected to very severe austerity measures leading to a slow down in local production and a consequent rise in unemployment. Other aspects include trade liberalization causing a flood of imported goods and leading to a false state of economic well-being for the elite few who depend on such foreign goods.

As a result of the fall in local productivity, many countries are unable to generate the resources needed to meet foreign donor loan repayments but these are readily rescheduled under the auspices of the IMF. This is clear indication of an ineffective structural adjustment programme although those responsible would rather ascribe this to other factors.

Structural adjustment programmes have generally created a temporary improvement in the standard of living for the implementing agencies and as such these groups tend to pursue the programmes irrespective of the hardship being experienced by the broader population.

It must be noted that the donors are not charitable institutions and have specific interests in making financial offers and agreeing to rescheduling of overdue debts.

Impact of structural adjustment programmes on social security

In view of these factors we must examine critically what effects these programmes tend to have on social security schemes. These are as follows:

- Retrenchment programmes, which are in reality redundancies, immediately increase the numbers of pensioners whilst reducing the active contributing workforce. This creates a severe financial impact on the sustainability of social security schemes.

- In most countries governments have been the major employers, and reductions in staff without any corresponding job creation result in high unemployment.

- Structural adjustment programmes have a short time frame and can, therefore, create financial imbalances for social security schemes.

Reformulation of structural adjustment programmes

It is becoming quite apparent that these programmes have not provided the long term sustainability required by most countries. It is essential, therefore, that basic country-specific solutions are sought which address the long term sustainability of the nations in distress. Such programmes should address the basic issues:

- improvement of agricultural yields by the peasant farmers who form the majority of the productive group;

- storage and preservation of such increased production;

- effective utilization of local raw materials into semi-processed materials for export;

- basic training for the broad group of manpower available as against expensive, high level training;

- mobilization of local financial resources towards effective infrastructure development to improve communications and to provide decent functional housing; and

- institutionalization of social security schemes to replace the disrupted traditional social security prevalent in rural areas.

In effect, it is essential for all of us to realize that the process of attempting to fine-tune these distressed economies is misplaced in view of the fact that the basic factors that can make the economy viable have not been put in place as yet.

We must resort to coarse-tuning as a first step before progressing to fine-tuning if we are to achieve any meaningful structural adjustment rather than temporary alleviation.

Framework and role of social security

In the future, as we realize the ineffectiveness of governments to grapple with basic economic development, the trend should be for social security to become independent and operate on a self-sustaining basis.

In this way, social security schemes will not only guarantee the future protection of members in old age but build up a reputation for job creation and economic growth through financial mediation.

In the long term governments are not likely to address the fundamental issues necessary for sustainable economic growth because of political short-term considerations which always pre-occupy them from one election to another. This short-term outlook is amplified further by the lurking danger of military interventions which must be included in governments' agendas.

The role emerging for social security institutions should be one that provides a stable base for implementing longer-term economic development plans in conjunction with the private sector.

In many instances, these plans have been clearly articulated by governments and the World Bank and do not have to be reformulated; but they must be prioritized for implementation instead of their being relegated to the archives.

Social security institutions can only assume this role of serving as a catalyst if they are fairly independent with regard to investment of funds. Under such circumstances, social security institutions can adopt the process of institution building with the private sector in order to provide the capacities required to implement these basic economic development plans. These plans should, in all cases, have a high human factor built into the objectives. A role of this nature ensures that social security institutions are not marginalized into payment of retirement pensions alone, but have an active impact in job creation to ensure the sustainability of the contract between generations.

9

A perspective from Central and Eastern Europe

Inara Bite
Deputy Minister of Welfare, Labour and Health
(Latvia)

The task of commenting on the reports of experts from the International Monetary Fund (IMF) and the World Bank, as well as those of other social security specialists, is a difficult one. I must explain that in Latvia there are currently no research institutions undertaking studies in the social security field and that I, as Deputy Minister for social welfare, am responsible for drawing up the social insurance budget and for determining income and expenditure within that budget. At the same time, however, my colleagues and I have to work together on planning the country's social policy. I therefore ask for the indulgence of the specialists if the theoretical basis of my views is inadequate.

It can be inferred from the contributions to this Symposium that the experts are well informed about the crisis facing social security in Central and Eastern Europe — and that they also appreciate that the totalitarian régimes have left a sorry inheritance for the new democratic states. The general trends in Eastern Europe have been very accurately described; but I must point out that developments are not all taking place at the same time in all parts of the region. For instance, developments which have already occurred in, say, Poland and Hungary have not yet occurred in the Baltic States — the latter won their independence at a later date. It is undeniable that the scope for social security reform depends on economic development. But economic development brings in its wake new sources of economic insecurity, which affect the social progress that has already been secured by individuals. Clearly, individuals and their families can only cope to a limited extent with the new problems that are arising. I cannot put the problem better than Professor James Schulz did in his report to the Symposium: "Too often policy advisers (and especially economists) give great weight to the long-term gains of markets but little weight to the short-term misery created in the process".

One of the most important questions which arises in connection with the reform of a social security system is that of the source of finance. In the countries of Central and Eastern Europe, with a few exceptions, benefits have been financed from the state budget. Mr Kopits from the IMF expressed the opinion that in the socialist planned economies the financing of benefits was to a substantial degree met from employer contributions to social insurance and paid into general revenue. However, this was not the case in the former USSR. There, social insurance contributions only covered sickness benefits. However, I must admit that in the surveys conducted during the period of Soviet government the situation was presented in such a manner as to suggest that insurance principles were working effectively.

Today, it is true to say that in most of the countries of Central and Eastern Europe social security schemes are being transformed into statutory social insurance systems. Professor Schulz has stated, not without some irony, that this is no more than an imitation of "Western practices". I think, however, that our belief in the principles of social insurance has other roots, which derive from the basic concept of social insurance, namely that financing is dependent essentially on contributions from insured persons and their employers, and that this offers the possibility of linking social insurance benefits with working life in the best possible way. Most of the countries with centrally planned economies have plenty of bitter experience of what happens when all social benefits are paid for out of the state budget. In our country we used to call this approach the "remainder principle".

The countries of Central and Eastern Europe are often criticized for setting the rates of social security contributions too high for their economies during the transition period. In several countries (Bulgaria and the Czech and Slovak Republics) the statutory contribution rates exceed 50 per cent. The criticism is well founded from the economic standpoint, since higher contribution rates have a negative effect on economic activity in a context of privatization of industry. However, I believe that in a situation of transition it is difficult to avoid measures of this kind if the state wishes to offer its citizens living conditions comprising some degree of human dignity.

The government of my country is endeavouring to follow the recommendations of the IMF and the World Bank. One of the conditions laid down by the IMF is the stabilization of the national currency. We have thus arrived at a situation where the average wage is below the minimum subsistence level; I leave the purchasing power of pensions to your imaginations. We are thus forced to attach great importance to public social assistance. It has to fill the gaps, while leaving open the question of the structure of the social benefits system.

But in social matters the psychological aspects must also be taken into account. It is not permissible to discard all the old concepts of pensions overnight in order to give legal force to a new system. This is precisely the case in the crisis we are currently facing. I think that the reform of the pensions system will have to be undertaken with the utmost caution in order to avoid a heightening of social tension within the community. Convincing proof of this can be obtained from one example − the effect of introducing a scheme of flat-rate pensions in my country. The pensioners who had had expectations of earnings-related pensions throughout their working lives − and had actually been receiving such pensions − were of course bitterly disillusioned; but, in addition, workers and officials currently in employment are now also losing faith in the principles of insurance − and that, from the social standpoint, is a serious loss.

Another subject of importance is the raising of pensionable ages. Some experts have stated that a retirement age of 60 for men and 55 for women is low by international standards and discriminates by sex. We agree that the pensionable age level is too low. But this problem must be examined in the context of the great diversity of problems in society as a whole. One must be aware of all the factors which have an influence in this field. They are:

- falling life expectancy;

- increasing unemployment; and

- the social tensions created by the current crisis.

We are prepared to increase the pensionable age in stages; but people must be given the choice of being able either to claim the full pension due to them or to apply for a partial pension only. As far as these three factors are concerned it should be mentioned that:

- The average life expectancy for men in Latvia is 62 years.

- The crucial problem regarding unemployment is that of determining which is the more rational course − to keep in employment the people who have the most difficulty in adapting to the new conditions of the market economy or to provide them with early retirement. Another problem arising in connection with unemployment is that if young people cannot find jobs on completing their specialist or university education, they may well never learn to work during their whole lives. I believe that the legislature in the Federal Republic of Germany had similar considerations in mind when it offered citizens of the five new Länder the possibility of taking retirement at age 55. In our view one cannot adopt the economically cheapest course in social matters; that approach can ultimately be of great cost.

Despite these concerns, I should not like to leave you with the impression that we are stubbornly clinging on to old concepts and rejecting the new ones proposed by the IMF and the World Bank. A year ago I had the good fortune to work for a week with Professor Robert Holzmann, an expert on Central and Eastern Europe. Following that week of work together, we submitted to the government a draft Bill concerning social insurance benefits which introduced substantial changes in the method of awarding sickness benefits. In that draft we followed consistently the recommendations of the World Bank. One must develop an interest — among employers and employees alike — in maintaining the health of working people. In the current crisis, when firms often have to shut down temporarily, it is actually in the interest of employers that their manual or white-collar workers should be entitled to claim sickness benefit. The Bill provides that, when a manual worker or salaried employee becomes incapacitated for work through illness, the employer must pay the benefit due in respect of the first three weeks. The insured person receives benefit from the social insurance scheme only if the illness lasts more than three weeks. In addition, the amount of sickness benefit is to be reduced. These legislative changes are also in line with the IMF's line of thinking. Other proposals are worthy of attention but difficult to put into practice — for example, the calculation of pension on the basis of wages during the entire working life. Unfortunately, the implementation of this proposal is impractical on account of the poor quality of the statistics for previous years. The establishment of a separate identification number for each insured person will, however, eventually be possible.

One can discuss these problems at length, and they have certainly been explored in the valuable contributions by leading social security specialists in greater depth than I have had time to do. I have therefore concentrated on the problems which seem most important in the situation in which my country — one of the post-communist countries — finds itself.

10

The need for institutional reform

Stanford G. Ross
Public Trustee and former Commissioner of the
Social Security Administration (United States)

I commend the ISSA for holding this Symposium on a subject of vital importance to social security professionals: how to make social security institutions
compatible with long-term economic development in a rapidly changing world.
I also commend the Secretary General for his emphasis at this meeting on the
urgent need today for critical evaluation of social security institutions in order
to focus on making the changes that are required to keep these institutions
viable for the future. In this spirit, I offer my own views on how constructive
change can best be undertaken in today's highly transitional world.

My views reflect my experiences as a practising lawyer, as a Public Trustee
and former Commissioner of the U.S. social security system, and as a consultant
to various governments around the world on legal, administrative and organizational issues. Based on my background of practical experience, I would emphasize the importance of increasing awareness of the limitations of social
security and the desirability of restricting social insurance approaches to those
that can be realistically delivered and are financially affordable. The strengths
of well-designed and well-executed social security programmes are well understood. Further, it is always useful to keep in mind the critical assistance social
security can give to the elderly, the disabled, children and families. Social
insurance can indeed increase political and social solidarity and alleviate poverty and hardship in a country. But it is the weaknesses of social security

institutions that most demand our attention today. There is a need to focus on reforms that will in fact improve institutions by taking fuller account of trade-offs inherent in social security systems and clearly establishing relative priorities to be accomplished by such systems. In many cases, the beginning of the reform process may be simply to lower expectations about what can actually be accomplished by social security systems, in order that those reduced expectations can be actually fulfilled.

Even where there are some successes, social security today is often a chronic source of government deficits and a financial burden that diminishes the ability of governments to perform generally for a country. Social security systems in developed countries generally are able to cope because of the accumulated economic strength that allows for adjustments to take place in an orderly and gradual fashion. But the situation in most of the developing world is far more uncertain.

The Americas illustrates this mixed picture very well. While benefiting many persons, traditional social insurance systems displaying European concepts inaugurated by Bismarck and others, have not fared well. The most dramatic innovations, as in Chile, were stimulated in fact by the collapse of traditional social insurance systems. Other places where troubled systems have not collapsed, like Argentina and Brazil, are attempting to take needed reform steps. Mexico has taken, and is taking, steps to keep social security viable. But in none of these places can the future of social security be secured without considerably more change and then achieving a record of satisfactory performance over a long period.

Eastern Europe and the former Soviet Union are only at the beginnings of reforming social security programmes. The public in these countries generally has been promised pension systems that are well beyond the means of governments. Large dependent populations must be supported at some level, while workers and businesses are given incentives to compete in free market societies. The future of existing social security institutions in these transition economies is in serious jeopardy, with all the problems that entails for political stability and social solidarity.

In Africa, the gaps between statutory schemes, modelled on concepts borrowed from the developed world, and actual operations are large. Indeed, there are no systems realistically operating in some places. In Asia, the picture is somewhat different because of the reliance in many places on provident funds which have functioned reasonably well. However, these generally are no more than compulsory savings plans. As they are converted to true social insurance systems, the perils are large. In brief, it is not clear what future developments will hold for social security institutions in the developing world.

Perhaps I overly emphasize the crisis aspects of the current situation. But if I do, it is mainly to set the stage for urging that the basic issue is having a realistic agenda for reform, one that can be accomplished if the political and professional communities surrounding social security in a country have the will to do it. In asking for realistic acknowledgment of the problems of social security, I would urge that the subject that needs to be focused on most is "institutional competency", that is, what can be done effectively and efficiently by social security in a country.

People in all countries today are suspicious of government. Populations the world over have been overthrowing governments, asking that governments be down-sized, and above all demanding that governments become more efficient, in the sense of imposing less taxes and producing greater services for the taxes collected. This new skepticism about government is a response to the fact that there have been too many failed promises and too much fraud, abuse and waste in governmental operations. Both the design and functioning of social programmes need to be reviewed in terms of today's environment of greater public suspicion of public management of social programmes.

I submit that whether one believes, as set forth at this Symposium, in social security to "the maximum degree possible" (ILO), or, "cost-effective", social programmes (IMF), or comprehensive multi-tiered systems (World Bank), or any other formulation, there is a need to improve the legal frameworks, administrative capacities and service delivery of social security systems the world over as a first step toward any of these design goals. The building of greater institutional competency is a prerequisite to substantive reform, whatever shape that reform is to take. Sound legal rules, efficient administration, and an organization that can properly implement reforms, are needed whatever a country opts for in the way of a substantive social security programme.

I would emphasize that the relationship between the design of programmes and the establishment of social security institutions is not a question of which comes first, the chicken or the egg. Clearly, design possibilities depend on institutional capacities to implement a reform programme. When dealing with social security, incremental change is best, which means that design options are limited by existing institutional capacities. Social security systems must learn to competently operate limited programmes before they can take on larger more comprehensive schemes.

Having made this plea for modest reform approaches based on incrementalism, I must acknowledge that this advice runs counter to the political impulse in most countries to promise a great deal and to design programs that go well beyond any possible capacity for implementation. The capacity for self-delusion among political actors in promising social benefits is limitless. As a consequence, social security professionals must provide a balance by emphasizing the need for realism in formulating reforms. Time is running short for social security institutions to achieve credibility by delivering benefits entirely in accord with those that are promised and not continually falling short on delivery. For social security to be at the centre of social provision in a country, it must be seen as a proven mechanism that accomplishes its goals. Public trust in the competency of social security institutions has to be earned by effective day-in and day-out performance over long periods.

Concrete steps that I would urge are that individual countries should do "realistic self-assessments" of their social security institutions with the use of independent monitors. It is very important that checks and balances be built into evaluations so that greater accountability and responsibility is encouraged. Financial management should be transparent, with strong requirements for current public reports and independent auditing of accounts. Social security institutions need to develop long-term strategic management plans that go along with long-term economic forecasts to ensure that social security systems will deliver promised benefits over long periods such as 50 or 60 years or more. There needs to be a great deal of emphasis on managerial integrity, financial accountability and sound operations.

ILO, IMF and World Bank technical assistance should emphasize programmes that are grounded in reforming institutions and increasing operational capacities. Assistance that is oriented toward design options generally should be secondary in today's world. Good design can only follow once there is a capacity to implement that design. Design options must be regarded as flowing from the ability to turn promises into operating programmes. A pragmatic approach to reform should underpin specific structural adjustment policies targeted on social security reform. By approaching social security reform in a practical fashion, the international institutions can help social security professionals in a country to create an environment in which vital reform work can have a reasonable chance to be accomplished.

ISSA and others could also help with this reform task by evolving detailed and specific standards for performance of social security institutions. Thus, there should be established objective measurements that are continually monitored. ISSA could have panels that provide guidelines that are then used in individual countries. For example, many well-run old-age and survivor programmes operate with expenses that are at one to two per cent of benefits paid. Well-run disability programmes can be found that operate at expense ratios that are less than five per cent. Most social security systems display costs that go well beyond these levels. Surely, there are guidelines that could be developed so that as a goal of a long-term strategic management plan a country could work toward achieving greater efficiencies. These are the kinds of issues that ISSA could be helpful with, since its members could bring their collective experience to bear to produce a practical framework for establishing objective measures for reform programmes to achieve.

Other specific areas in which there could be useful work would involve the comparative advantage of having contributions collected by social security agencies or by the tax authorities. There are examples of successful operations under both approaches. However, there could be efficiencies for developing countries in which tax collection is further advanced than social security collection in combining these functions in one agency.

New technologies, particularly computers and telecommunications, are also a fertile area for cooperative work among countries. Examples can be found of both overuse and underuse. There are examples of conflicts of interest in procurement and deployment. All of these pitfalls can be avoided if foreseen and careful planning based on proven experience is undertaken.

Consolidating special pension arrangements, as for government employees and the military, is also an area where much can be learned from other systems. The United States and Japan recently successfully integrated separate systems, and other countries can also be looked at as models for working toward universal arrangements that are fairer and more efficient.

The use of legal arrangements such as trust funds or other fiduciary arrangements to protect beneficiaries' and workers' interests can be enhanced. Here again studies across countries could be important to making valuable expertise more widely available to countries that need to develop legal safeguards for social security programs.

Another area where ISSA could help would be in adapting the emerging concept of total quality management, which is sweeping the world with respect to private sector companies, to social security operations. Total quality management includes among other things energizing organizations from the top through the bottom to deliver services more efficiently and more effectively. Governments in some places are adapting these concepts to the public sector, and it would be useful to have this knowledge made available more widely to social security institutions.

Assuming that better institutional capacities can be produced in the years ahead, I would also submit that now is the time to begin to think creatively about the design of programmes and to review old formulations in terms of the new world that is emerging. For example, legitimacy in social security may be found in more limited systems than those that prevail today in most of the OECD countries. Governmental approaches that are too expansive may tend to crowd out complementary private pension approaches or supplemental voluntary saving approaches. Both public and private systems need to be harmonized. ISSA members can learn valuable lessons from one another if they abandon the notion that social security is always a "solution" to problems and recognize that in the world we live in today social security is often itself the "problem" that has to be solved by a combination of public and private approaches.

New, more viable, forms for social security can be found if social security professionals lead the way. There can be coherence and cooperation among public and private approaches. These two approaches do not have to be seen as competitive. A balanced approach may well be necessary that looks at all the alternatives in a particular country for limited private systems as well as limited public systems, all harnessed to greater social purposes that are realistically defined.

It is also important to recognize that emulation of other countries' social security systems is often a mistake. Design options and institutional forms that may work very well for one country may not be viable in another. There has been far too much emphasis to date on developed country forms in developing countries. My own belief is that the history of social security is not a clear path of progress, with antecedents in indigenous sharing among participants in traditional communities and organized societal responses to industrialization. Rather, it has been more of a random walk through various political cultures in an attempt to mitigate social problems through collective approaches that sometimes work and sometimes do not. It is by no means clear that existing social security institutions will prosper in the 21st century. Just as society in the 21st century will be quite different that what we have experienced in the 20th century, social security will have to be different. Many of the 19th and 20th century forms that have been carried forward to today need to be rethought and adapted. This is a challenge social security professionals have to successfully meet to keep social security viable.

Social security institutions everywhere today are under intense scrutiny and in need of demonstrating legitimacy. Greater professionalism is required if they are to develop the institutional capacities to survive. The mission of ISSA to "defend, promote and develop social security" can best be accomplished by careful, technically-oriented work based on increasing institutional competency. That is a basic challenge for ISSA in the years ahead.

11

Concluding comments

James H. Schulz
**Professor at Brandeis University (United States)
and ISSA Consultant**

Well, we have reached the end of the Symposium and certainly I have heard no-one dispute the fact that we are at a very critical juncture with regard to issues about social security structural reform and development. There are many differences, however, in how to approach the issues and in our opinions about what the true nature of the problem is.

In planning for this Symposium, the ISSA had some difficulty in trying to adequately cover both the rather unique and important developments and economic changes in the former Communist countries — such as those discussed in the report that you heard from Ms. Bite from Latvia — and the on-going problems in the less developed countries — as indicated in the discussion by Mr. Dei, for example. While the history and the nature of the situation in these two general groups of countries is in a very fundamental way quite different, I think that the basic issues that have to be addressed are very similar, and I think that most of the people who have spoken today have tried, in one way or another, to address those basic issues.

I just very quickly want to look at three issues we discussed that seem to me to be critical. I begin first with the one that we heard least about, the issue of access or coverage. I believe that there is a significant problem in many countries with regard to broadening coverage. As we heard from Mr. Saldain at one point in his remarks: "In many countries the social protection system reproduces the power structure of the country". Such statements remind us that when we look at the coverage question, a big part of the issue we have to deal with is the political will of a particular country to extend its coverage broadly within the population. There are, of course, more technical issues which have been struggled with over the years and these are very real problems. I mentioned some of them in my paper. However, those of you who administer programmes and are interested in broadening the coverage know much more about them and know just how difficult they are. Mr. Engo from Cameroon mentioned a special problem with regard to coverage when he suggested that the dynamics of structural adjustment in his country had actually made it much more difficult to progress the country's goals with regard to broadening coverage.

Mr. Gillion at the very beginning of this session made a very strong statement calling for the expansion of social protection mechanisms (which I am sure most of us would agree with). But, at this session today, no-one came up with a generally acceptable strategy for undertaking this broad expansion. As you know, the ISSA has looked at the question again and again over the years and has given it a lot of thought, but (again) it has not come up with very good answers. It seems to me that we have to acknowledge that, given the current general economic crisis, this issue of coverage is more important than ever — no matter how difficult it is to deal with. Yet, given the crisis, it's the most likely issue to be ignored. I think in part the discussion today ignored this issue. It is time for the ISSA to revisit this question in a very serious way.

This leads me to the second issue: the question of adequacy and equity. One approach that is receiving a lot of attention around the world is that more emphasis should be given to government programmes that focus on the poor, leaving the economic support of the non-poor primarily to the private sector. Now, you will immediately recognize this as a debate that has taken place over many years. It is in large part, the issue of "universalism versus means-testing". Some have proposed, although no-one directly today, that we should shift to providing broader coverage and improved adequacy through social assistance programmes. I gave a lot of attention to this issue in my paper because I think it's such an important issue. I want to assure the delegate from Australia (given his comments) that if my statements sounded extreme, they are a reflection of a lot of thought and study over the years. It is important to clarify that the type of social assistance scheme that I was talking about in my paper is not the Australian "age pension" scheme. The system in Australia is very interesting, very complex and (I know) very popular in that country. But it is also very atypical of means-tested benefit schemes around the world. And with regard to the question of incentives, I believe that the Australian system does have serious savings incentive problems and serious problems with regard to discouraging labour force participation.

The other option we discussed today with regard to adequacy and equity is the multi-pillared approach. Mr. Vittas provided us with a very useful description of the potential links between the basic public pensions, supplemental pensions from the private sector and voluntary savings in his three country examples — showing us how one might approach building better multi-pillared systems. The differences in opinions, of course, will be on where the emphasis should be with regard to the pillars, and I sensed that there is some significant differences among participants on this matter. Certainly, as you well know, there is increasing interest in harnessing market mechanisms to deal with social welfare needs. But, as Mr. Vittas pointed out, and I think quite correctly, "good" private programmes depend fundamentally on "good" government (in terms of necessary supervision and regulation). So the distinction between public and private approaches becomes very muddied. Choosing an emphasis is not as easy as some people think. And if a country seeks to shift emphasis, I think it must first pay a great deal of attention to history and learn what history has to tell us about these options.

Finally, let us focus on the issue which received the most attention today — the issue of implementation. Mr. Kopits made a very strong statement. He said the main goal of social security reform is cost-effectiveness and Mr. Ross reminded us that there is too much fraud, abuse and waste in programmes throughout the world. Well, how are we to deal with the serious implementation problems that arise? How are we to make these programmes more efficient and more effective? Admittedly to oversimplify, I think there are two approaches: one is privatization together with government regulation; the other is to push greater openness with regard to the operation of government-run programmes — that is to "turn the flashlight on them" to let the people know how they are actually operating and the extent to which they are not operating appropriately. Mr. Vittas suggested that we should shift towards privately administered programmes for that part of the pillar above the basic pension but, as he pointed out, the success of that still depends in a fundamental way on some amount of government regulation and the quality of that government regulation. Mr. Ross called for independent monitoring and for long-term strategic management plans with regard to government-run social security programmes. All seem to me to be suggestions worthy of serious consideration. Finally, all the papers seemed to suggest, and I heard nothing contrary from the commentators, that we do not have to follow one particular path of reform, but that we should follow various paths simultaneously with regard to improving the various pillars.

There is, of course, no global answer to the questions the Symposium sought to address. Obviously, we must continue to move, however, from the very general to a more specific analysis of the questions covered by our meeting. And we can be sure that follow-up will be one of the major concerns of the ISSA. I am certain, therefore, that this is just the very beginning of a continuing dialogue with regard to this most important topic.

DATE DUE   L.-Brault

Bibliofiche 297B